STOLEN LIBERTY

ECHOES OF A MANDATE

Brett Coon

STOLEN LIBERTY: ECHOES OF A MANDATE

Copyright © 2024 by BRETT COON

DEDICATION

For my son, and for all those who live in a world that doesn't always hear their voice.

TABLE OF CONTENTS

FOREWORD

I never thought I'd be the kind of person whose life could be swept aside, marked "unimportant" by the powers that be. But in this world, I've learned how quickly things can change. My story isn't unique. In fact, it's all too common for people like me— ordinary people just trying to make it through each day, caring for family, working hard, wanting the same chance as anyone else to live and be free.

This book, *Stolen Liberty: Echoes of a Mandate,* is made up of stories that are chillingly familiar to me and so many others. It captures, in raw detail, the quiet and devastating ways policies can reshape lives. Reading it, you may think these tales are just fiction. I assure you, they are closer to truth than anyone would like to admit.

When you're on the outside of power, the decisions made in distant rooms by people who don't know your name or your struggles are the ones that end up defining your life. A law passes, and suddenly you can't afford medicine for your child. A policy changes, and the job you rely on no longer has any protection. An ideal becomes a mandate, and the rights you took for granted start slipping away. In a world where laws grow harsher and compassion becomes scarce, people like me live with the consequences every single day.

Stolen Liberty speaks for us. It gives voice to our fears, our quiet heartbreak, our resilience, and our sense of betrayal. For everyone reading this book, I ask you to remember: These stories may be fiction, but they hold a powerful truth. They remind us that no one is immune, that every policy is personal, and that there are real people behind every statistic.

May these voices reach those in power, and may they also remind you that standing up for one another—no matter how big or small—is the most human thing we can do. Because in the end, these are our lives, our families, our futures, and they deserve to be protected.

– A friend.

skimmed through a newspaper, occasionally sipping his drink without taking his eyes off the print.

Michael felt a disconnect—a jarring dissonance between the gravity of what he was witnessing and the indifferent bubble encapsulating everyone else. He tightened his grip on the mug, the ceramic cool against his skin, grounding him amidst the surreal tableau.

The camera zoomed in on the young woman, capturing the subtle tremor in her lips as she prepared to speak. The courtroom seemed to hold its breath, and Michael found himself doing the same.

On the screen, the camera zoomed in on the young woman as she stood at the defendant's table, her frail figure dwarfed by the imposing architecture of the courtroom. The harsh overhead lights illuminated every bruise and cut on her face, each one a silent testament to the violence she had endured. Her left eye was swollen nearly shut, and a deep purple contusion marred her cheekbone. Despite the physical injuries, it was the emptiness in her gaze that struck Michael the most—a hollow despair that seemed to drain the color from her surroundings.

The prosecutor stepped forward, his crisp suit and polished demeanor a stark contrast to the woman's disheveled appearance. He adjusted his glasses deliberately before addressing the court. "Your Honor, ladies and gentlemen of the jury," he began, his voice resonating with practiced authority. "We are here to hold the defendant accountable for the negligent loss of an innocent life—a life that was entrusted to her care."

The young woman gripped the edge of the table, her knuckles turning white. Her hands trembled visibly, and Michael could almost feel the tremor coursing through her body. She opened her mouth to speak, but no words came out, only a silent gasp as she struggled to find her voice.

"Miss Turner," the prosecutor continued, turning his gaze directly upon her, "do you deny that your actions led to the demise of your unborn child?"

She swallowed hard, her throat constricting. "I... I tried to protect my baby," she managed to say, her voice barely above a whisper, her hands flying to her abdomen as if the very act could bring her child back to her. "He pushed me down the stairs. I didn't—"

"Objection," the prosecutor interrupted sharply. "The defendant is attempting to deflect responsibility by casting blame on an innocent man."

In the gallery, a figure shifted—her boyfriend, impeccably dressed, his expression a mask of concern that didn't quite reach his eyes. He sat flanked by supporters, exuding an air of vindication. Michael felt a surge of anger rise within him, his jaw clenching involuntarily.

The judge nodded. "Sustained. The defendant will refrain from unfounded accusations."

Tears welled in the young woman's eyes, spilling over to trace paths down her bruised cheeks. "I'm telling the truth," she pleaded, her gaze darting desperately around the courtroom. "Please, you have to believe me."

Her mother sat in the front row, her face etched with anguish. She clutched a handkerchief to her mouth, stifling sobs that threatened to escape. Beside her, the father stared straight ahead, his eyes glistening but unblinking, his hands balled into tight fists on his knees.

Michael's heart ached at the sight. He glanced around the diner, wondering if anyone else was witnessing this travesty. A few patrons glanced at the television, their expressions indifferent before returning to their meals. The disconnect was palpable, a chasm between his mounting despair and the casual normalcy surrounding him.

Back in the courtroom, the prosecutor pressed on. "The evidence clearly shows negligence on the part of the defendant. Medical records indicate alcohol in her system, and witnesses attest to frequent domestic disturbances. This was not an isolated incident but a pattern of reckless behavior."

"That's not true!" she cried out, her voice breaking. "He was the one who hurt me. He threatened me. I was trying to leave to protect my baby."

"Enough," the judge declared, his tone icy. "Miss Turner, you have been warned about outbursts."

She recoiled as if struck, her shoulders hunching inward. The weight of the courtroom's gaze bore down upon her, and she seemed to shrink under its pressure.

Michael felt a burning frustration. How could they dismiss her so easily? The truth was plain to see, etched across every bruise and scar.

The prosecutor turned to the jury. "Ladies and gentlemen, we cannot allow personal tragedies to cloud our judgment. The law is clear. The loss of an innocent life demands justice."

A hush fell over the courtroom as the judge prepared to deliver the verdict. The tension was palpable, a coiled spring ready to snap. The young woman closed her eyes, her lips moving silently as if in prayer.

"In the case of the State versus Emily Turner," the judge intoned, "this court finds the defendant guilty of negligent homicide."

A muted gasp rippled through the courtroom. Emily's eyes flew open, disbelief and despair warring in her expression.

"Sentencing will proceed immediately," the judge continued, his face devoid of emotion. "Given the severity of the crime and its impact on societal values, I hereby sentence you to death."

Her mother let out a wail, collapsing against her husband, who held her tightly as tears streamed down his own face. Emily shook her head violently. "No, please! I'm innocent! You have to believe me!"

Two guards approached, their expressions impassive as they took her by the arms. She struggled weakly, her pleas growing more frantic. "Don't do this! Please! I didn't do anything!"

Michael's hands balled into fists, his nails digging into his palms. He felt utterly powerless, a spectator to an unthinkable injustice.

The camera panned to the boyfriend, who stood up smoothly, adjusting his tie with a subtle smirk. Reporters swarmed around him as he exited the courtroom.

"Mr. Davis, do you have any comment on the verdict?" a journalist pressed.

He offered a solemn nod. "It's a tragic situation," he said, feigning sorrow. "But justice has been served. I hope this brings some closure and allows everyone to heal."

Michael nearly spat in disgust. The man's insincerity was blatant, yet no one seemed to notice—or care.

The television returned to the studio, where the news anchor shifted to a lighter topic without missing a beat. "In other news, the annual spring festival is set to begin this weekend, promising fun for the whole family."

Michael looked around the diner once more. A child laughed as he blew bubbles into his chocolate milk. An elderly couple shared a quiet conversation, smiles softening their features. Life continued, undisturbed.

He felt a crushing sense of isolation, as if he were the only one awake in a world content to sleepwalk through tragedy.

Michael sat transfixed, his gaze locked onto the flickering screen as the young woman was led away, her anguished cries muted by the diner's ambient noise. The camera lingered on her tear-streaked face, capturing the raw devastation that seemed to reach through the screen and grip his very soul. Her parents were restrained by court officers, their faces contorted in grief, mouths open in silent screams. The boyfriend stood in the background, a satisfied smirk tugging at the corners of his mouth—a serpent basking in the chaos he had sown.

A cold numbness spread through Michael's limbs. He felt as if he were submerged underwater, the sounds around him distorted and distant. How could such a blatant miscarriage of justice unfold before everyone's eyes, yet provoke no reaction?

He tore his gaze from the television, his eyes darting around the diner. A teenage girl snapped a selfie, adjusting her hair to catch the light just right. A group of college students debated the merits of the latest smartphone, their voices animated and carefree. An older man chuckled at the comic strip in his newspaper, shaking his head in amused disbelief.

"Doesn't anyone see this?" Michael whispered, his voice barely audible even to himself.

He glanced back at the screen just as the broadcast cut to a press conference outside the courthouse. The boyfriend stepped up to a cluster of microphones, flanked by lawyers who exuded practiced sympathy. Reporters jostled for position, shouting questions that blurred into an incoherent roar.

"Justice was served today," the boyfriend declared, his tone measured but tinged with feigned sorrow. "While it's a tragic situation, I hope we can all begin the healing process."

Michael's stomach churned. The audacity of the man's performance was sickening—a predator cloaked in the veneer of victimhood. He looked around again, desperate to find even a flicker of shared outrage, but the diner's patrons remained ensnared in their own worlds.

A sharp laugh erupted from the booth behind him. "No way! She did not say that!" one woman exclaimed, her eyes gleaming with gossip-fueled excitement.

"Excuse me," Michael called out, his voice strained. The woman glanced at him briefly, eyebrows raised, before turning back to her companion without acknowledgment.

He felt a surge of frustration boiling over into anger. Grabbing the remote, he turned up the volume, the sudden increase drawing annoyed glances. The news had shifted to a statement from the Leader, his imposing figure filling the screen.

"Citizens," the Leader began, his voice smooth and authoritative. "Today, our nation took a necessary step in upholding the values we hold dear. The sanctity of life is paramount, and those who threaten it will face the full weight of our justice system."

Michael's grip tightened on the remote, his knuckles whitening. The hypocrisy was palpable, each word dripping with calculated manipulation. He could feel the walls closing in, the air thick with a complacency that suffocated any spark of dissent.

"Hey, can you turn that down?" someone called from across the room.

Michael spun around to see a man scowling at him over a plate of untouched food. "Some of us are trying to enjoy our meal," the man added pointedly.

"Enjoy your meal?" Michael echoed, disbelief coloring his tone. "An innocent woman was just condemned, and you care more about the volume on the TV?"

The man's expression hardened. "Look, buddy, it's not our problem. Keep it down."

A murmur of agreement rippled through the diner. Faces turned away, eyes avoiding his. The waitress approached cautiously, her smile strained. "Is everything okay here?" she asked softly.

"No, everything is not okay," Michael replied, his voice rising despite himself. "How can you all sit here and ignore what's happening? Don't you see the injustice?"

She glanced at the screen and then back at him, her eyes reflecting a mix of concern and impatience. "I understand it's upsetting, but maybe you should calm down."

"Calm down?" He stood up abruptly, the stool scraping loudly against the tiled floor. "That's the problem—everyone's too calm! We're numb to what's right in front of us!"

The manager emerged from the back, his gaze stern. "Sir, I'm going to have to ask you to lower your voice or leave."

Michael stared at the manager, the weight of the man's words pressing down on him like a physical force. The diner's fluorescent lights seemed to grow harsher, casting stark shadows that accentuated the apathy etched into the faces around him. His heart hammered in his chest, a mix of rage and despair twisting inside him like a storm ready to break.

"Lower my voice?" he repeated, his tone edged with disbelief. "An innocent woman is about to be executed, and you want me to be quiet?"

Murmurs rippled through the diner. A few patrons shifted uncomfortably in their seats, while others pointedly avoided eye contact, focusing intently on their plates or phones. The clatter of silverware resumed, a discordant soundtrack to Michael's mounting anguish.

"Sir," the manager began, his expression a strained mask of professionalism, "I understand that you're upset, but you're disturbing our other customers. Please, either calm down or I'll have to ask you to leave."

Michael's gaze swept the room, searching desperately for a glimmer of shared humanity. "Doesn't anyone care?" he implored, his voice cracking. "Can't you see what's happening? This isn't justice—it's a travesty!"

A young woman near the window glanced up briefly, her eyes reflecting a flicker of sympathy before she lowered her head again, her fingers tightening around her coffee mug. An older man at the counter shook his head subtly, muttering something under his breath about "troublemakers."

The waitress who had served Michael earlier approached cautiously, her hands clasped tightly together. "Maybe you should step outside for some air," she suggested softly. "It might help."

He looked at her, noticing the slight tremor in her voice, the way her gaze darted nervously toward the manager. "Is that it?" he asked bitterly. "Just step outside, take a deep breath, and pretend everything's fine?"

She opened her mouth to respond but faltered, words failing her.

Michael felt a hollowness opening up inside him, a chasm of isolation that threatened to swallow him whole. The television continued its relentless broadcast, now displaying images of smiling officials shaking hands, the caption reading: "Justice Served. Nation Moves Forward."

"Nation moves forward," he whispered, a bitter taste coating his tongue. "At what cost?"

The manager's patience was wearing thin. "I'm sorry, but if you won't keep your voice down, I'll have to call the authorities."

"Authorities?" Michael echoed, a cold realization settling in. "You mean the same authorities that let a murderer walk free while sentencing his victim to death?"

Gasps fluttered around the diner. The manager stiffened, his eyes narrowing. "That's enough. Leave now, or I'll make the call."

For a moment, Michael considered staying, pushing further, forcing them all to face the uncomfortable truth. But the exhaustion was overwhelming, the weight of his solitary protest crushing. Shoulders slumping, he raised his hands in a gesture of surrender. "Fine," he said quietly. "I'll go."

He grabbed his jacket from the back of his chair, the fabric heavy in his grasp. As he turned to leave, his eyes met those of the young woman by the window once more. This time, she held his gaze, a silent apology shimmering in her eyes. He offered a faint, sad smile before stepping toward the exit.

The bell above the door jingled mockingly as he pushed it open, the chill of the evening air hitting him like a slap. Outside, the city thrummed with life—cars honking, pedestrians bustling along the sidewalks, neon signs flickering with relentless cheer. The world moved on, indifferent to the injustices playing out within it.

Michael stood on the sidewalk, the diner's warm glow behind him a stark contrast to the cold detachment he felt all around. He shoved his hands into his pockets, his fingers brushing against loose change and crumpled receipts—mundane remnants of a life that suddenly felt inconsequential.

A knot tightened in his throat as the weight of his helplessness settled in. One man against the tide, his voice drowned out by the overwhelming current of apathy. The faces of the young woman and her grieving parents flashed through his mind—their pain, their despair, the finality of a system that had failed them utterly.

He tilted his head back, staring up at the night sky. The stars were obscured by the city lights, a hazy glow that masked the vastness beyond. "Is anyone watching?" he whispered, his breath forming a pale cloud in the crisp air. "Does anyone care?"

Michael's shoulders sagged. The urge to scream, to rail against the suffocating indifference, welled up inside him, but the words caught in his throat. What was the point? Who would listen?

With a heavy sigh, he began to walk, each step feeling like an effort against an unseen force.

TWO

The clinic was empty...

Tom's cane tapped against the cold tile floor, each step echoing in the hollow silence, louder than he'd remembered. Each step sent a sharp jolt up his leg, the kind of pain he'd long since accepted as part of himself, though it still hit like a slow, twisting blade.

He glanced around the waiting room. Rows of plastic chairs stretched before him, their seats pockmarked from use, once filled with familiar faces. Now they sat vacant beneath the dim, flickering lights, which buzzed faintly, casting harsh, uneven shadows that seemed to settle in every corner. A chill lingered in the air, as if the warmth and humanity of the place had faded alongside the people who'd once filled it.

Tom's gaze fell on a single piece of paper, hastily taped to the counter. The message was scrawled in cold, detached letters: "This facility is permanently closed." The words seemed to hang in the air, stark and final, more brutal than the dull ache in his spine. He blinked, feeling a strange tightness in his chest as he struggled to make sense of it.

For a moment, memories flashed before him: the waiting room full of voices, nods of silent understanding, the gentle hum of conversation that once made this place feel almost like a second home—a refuge where his suffering was seen, shared, and understood. Now, the silence pressed down on him, as if every wall were drawing inward, leaving him alone with the weight of his pain and the emptiness of broken promises.

Tom stared at the sign, feeling as though the letters were dissolving before his eyes, each word blurring into the next. *This facility is permanently closed.* He mouthed the words, barely registering their meaning. It felt impossible, like something he'd wake up from. But the cold tile under his feet and the dull ache in his leg tethered him to the moment, forcing the reality to sink in slowly, painfully.

A pulse of pain shot up his leg, sharper than usual, and he gripped his cane until his knuckles whitened, fighting to keep steady. Every nerve in his body seemed to scream in protest, a reminder of every sacrifice he'd made, every sleepless night, every friend he'd buried. His chest tightened, and his breaths came in shallow gasps, struggling against the weight pressing down on him, as if the walls themselves were closing in.

A voice broke through the silence, jolting him. "Excuse me, sir." A young security guard stood nearby, his hands clasped tightly in front of him, his gaze flicking away as though afraid to meet Tom's eyes. "I'm afraid the clinic's closed. Permanently." The words cut through Tom like a blade, each syllable laced with finality, stripping away any hope that this was a mistake.

"They… they closed it?" Tom's voice came out hoarse, barely a whisper. He didn't recognize it—it sounded small, like someone else's voice, beaten down. "But… I can't make it to the main VA. It's forty miles out." He struggled to explain, his words stumbling, pleading. But the guard just shifted awkwardly, eyes dropping to the floor.

"I'm… I'm sorry, sir," the guard muttered, his apology as empty as the clinic itself. It was clear he didn't mean it, not really. He couldn't; he didn't understand. He was just trying to get through this moment, trying to avoid the pain that radiated from Tom like an unspoken wound.

Then came the final insult, the words Tom had heard a thousand times, words that had long since lost any meaning. "Thank you for your service."

The phrase felt like a slap, hollow and cheap, an empty reflex from someone who'd never faced anything close to what he and his friends had endured. Those words had once meant something—back when they'd come from people who understood, who could look him in the eye. Now, they were just noise, reminders of a society that had moved on and left him behind.

He nodded slowly, his grip on the cane tightening as he turned away. Each step was heavy, a dull ache that seemed to grow with every inch between him and the place he'd once counted on. Each painful step a reminder of promises broken, and the emptiness left behind.

That night, Tom lay awake in his dim apartment, the sounds of the empty clinic and the guard's words echoing in his mind. Each pulse of pain in his leg was like a nagging reminder of everything he'd lost—the friends he'd buried, the years of service he'd given. He'd clung to the clinic as a lifeline, a place where he didn't have to bear it alone. Now, it was gone, and the loneliness gnawed at him, kept him from sleep, left him staring at the dark ceiling as the hours dragged on. When he finally dozed off, it was only to wake up, body aching, knowing he still had to try to fill his prescription.

The next day, Tom made his way to the pharmacy, each step a painful battle as his spine throbbed with a relentless ache, the pain radiating through his legs like jagged shards. He clutched his prescription tightly, holding it as one might a lifeline, a faint hope that maybe, somehow, he could find relief.

When he reached the counter, the pharmacist greeted him with a detached smile, her eyes already flitting past him, focusing on the next person in line before she even scanned his prescription.

"That'll be $600," she said, her voice flat, the words rattling off as though she were quoting the price of gum. Tom blinked, the words hitting him like a punch to the gut.

"Six… six hundred?" He felt his voice waver, thin and weak, barely his own. "But… this was covered." His gaze bore into her, searching her face for some sign that he'd heard wrong.

The pharmacist gave a slight, impersonal shrug, her fingers tapping the screen before her. "It doesn't seem your provider covers this anymore, sir," she replied, glancing back at the line, her voice routine and matter-of-fact.

He opened his mouth, but no words came, only a desperate, strangled sound. His throat tightened, the edges of his vision blurring. "I… I can't afford that. I need these. You… you don't understand."

The pharmacist paused, her face softening just a fraction, but she still wouldn't meet his eyes. "I'm sorry. I really am," she said, her tone lowering as though to sound empathetic, though the words felt rehearsed. Behind him, the line shifted, and Tom noticed a young mother glancing over, her child tugging at her sleeve, her own face etched with stress. He could see the weight of her burdens too, and he knew his plea would change nothing.

The pharmacist looked back at him with something close to pity in her eyes, but even that felt insincere. She sighed softly before offering the same phrase he'd heard over and over, one that felt as empty as his pockets. "Thank you for your service."

Her words cut through him like cold steel, a hollow echo that left him feeling more alone than before. With a heavy nod, he turned and left, his legs trembling as he walked, the bitterness clawing up his throat. The door swung shut behind him, the sterile light of the pharmacy replaced by the cold grip of the street. The prescription, now worthless, hung in his hand, a reminder of all he could no longer have.

Back in his apartment that night, Tom sat in the dim light, surrounded by the prescription bottles he'd managed to cling to over the years, each one now empty, each one a small lifeline that seemed to slip further away. He felt the walls closing in, a hollowness settling in his chest that grew heavier with every passing hour. He thought of Eddie, another vet who understood the weight of those broken promises, the isolation that seemed to deepen every day. Eddie would understand. They'd leaned on each other before. And so, the next day, with a sense of desperation, Tom made his way to Eddie's apartment, hoping for a spark of connection.

One day, in a rare moment of strength, Tom pulled himself together and made his way to Eddie's apartment. Eddie was a fellow vet, someone who'd been through it all, just like him. They'd shared stories late into the night, swapped meds when they could, and laughed at dark jokes only they could understand. The thought of Eddie's raspy laugh and warm camaraderie was the one thing that gave Tom the strength to push forward that day, despite the throbbing ache in his leg and the hollow feeling in his chest.

When he reached Eddie's door, he paused, leaning on his cane as he caught his breath. The hallway was still, too still, and a faint smell of dust and stale air lingered, the kind that settles when a place has been untouched. He knocked, the sound sharp in the quiet, but there was no response. Tom's stomach tightened, a strange unease settling over him as he tried again, his knuckles rapping louder.

The door stayed closed, the windows behind it dark.

"Are you looking for Eddie?" A voice behind him made him turn. A neighbor, an older woman with worry lines etched deep into her face, stood wringing her hands, her mouth pressed into a tight line. She lowered her gaze to the floor as she spoke, her voice soft, almost reluctant. "He… passed away quietly in his sleep last week."

Tom's breath caught, his grip tightening on the cane. "His… his heart gave out?" he asked, his voice barely a whisper, struggling to grasp her words.

The woman nodded, her eyes holding a quiet sorrow, as though she'd seen it all happen and was powerless to stop it. "They say his heart just… gave out," she murmured, her gaze falling to the floor, her words carrying an unspoken sadness that mirrored his own. "It happens with men like him. They… well, they just fade."

Tom nodded, though his mind felt like it was in a fog, each word hitting him like a blow. Eddie's heart hadn't just given out; it had been worn down, whittled away piece by piece by the lack of support, by every night spent alone, by every promise broken. Another life, quietly erased, another friend reduced to a memory.

He turned slowly, each step back to his apartment feeling heavier, Eddie's raspy laugh echoing faintly in his mind like a ghost, a sound that grew fainter with each stride. When he finally reached his door, he collapsed onto his bed, clutching his aching shoulder, fighting back the tears that clawed up his throat, desperate to escape.

As he lay there, he knew, deep down, that Eddie wouldn't be the last. They were all like that now—just shadows fading quietly, men who had given everything, who had bled and broken for their country, left with nothing but the dim memories of what they'd once been.

The days passed, each one bleeding into the next, an endless stretch of silent, empty hours. Tom's world grew smaller, confined to his dim apartment, the shadows stretching long over the empty bottles on his table. His tremors worsened, each spasm a reminder of what he couldn't afford, of the help that was once close but now felt unreachable. Nights became long, sleepless stretches, hours blending into each other as he lay in bed, staring at the faint cracks in the ceiling, feeling the weight of his body pressing down, growing heavier by the day.

He often found himself holding the yellowed photographs from his days in uniform, the young man in the picture looking back at him with a fire in his eyes, a pride he barely remembered. That face—his own face—felt foreign now, like a person he'd only met once, a long time ago. The strength, the purpose, it had all been stripped away, leaving only a hollow ache in his chest.

One night, as he sat alone by the window, the pain in his chest grew sharp, a crushing, suffocating weight that seemed to squeeze every last breath from his lungs. His fingers curled around the edge of the armchair, knuckles white, as he struggled to pull himself upright, his breaths coming in shallow gasps. The agony twisted inside him, relentless, until he could no longer sit still. He stumbled to the door, gripping the frame as his legs trembled beneath him, his vision blurring, the faint outlines of the room fading into a hazy darkness.

The cold air hit him like a slap as he stepped out into the empty street, the chill biting through his skin, sinking deep into his bones. He looked down the road, his gaze unfocused, the familiar buildings and streetlights blurring together, blending into the night. The world around him continued, indifferent, the distant hum of traffic a faint reminder that life moved on, oblivious to his presence, to his suffering.

Each step forward felt like an impossible feat, the weight of his past pulling him down, grounding him to the concrete beneath his feet. His breath came in shallow, ragged gasps as he took another step, and then another, each one slower than the last. His body ached, every muscle heavy with exhaustion, as if he were carrying the ghosts of his friends, the memories of every sacrifice he'd made.

Finally, his legs gave out, and he sank onto the cold concrete, his hands splaying out to catch himself. He could feel the roughness of the pavement under his palms, the cold seeping through his bones, chilling him from the inside out. He tilted his head back, staring up at the sky, the stars hidden behind the city's bright, indifferent lights.

As his vision dimmed, he felt a strange clarity settle over him, a painful understanding that there would be no one. No hand reaching out, no voice offering comfort, no refuge from the silence that surrounded him. Just darkness, the quiet descent of a man who had given everything, only to be met with nothing in return.

The street lay silent, empty, the faint glow of the streetlights casting a pale halo around his still form. The world around him moved on, unaware, unseeing, and he allowed himself to sink into that darkness, abandoned, no longer fighting, letting go of the struggle he had carried alone for so long.

THREE

The pantry shelves were almost bare. Martha ran her fingers over the rough wood, feeling the empty spaces where cans of soup, bags of rice, and jars of peanut butter had once been. She turned and looked at the calendar on the wall, each day of the month crossed out in black ink, one by one, leading to the day that had changed everything. The first of the month had once meant relief, when SNAP benefits would reload, carrying them through to the next month. But this month, the benefits had been cut.

A single letter had arrived instead, signed by some official who felt like a phantom, informing her of "necessary redistribution" under the new mandate. It had been clinical, cold, with a line about "patience in difficult times," as if a few simple words could fill an empty cupboard. The letter had suggested budgeting "wisely" and "prioritizing resources," but her resources were already stretched to the bone. Patience and prioritizing weren't enough to fill a pantry or keep Arthur's body strong.

She turned back to Arthur, slumped in his armchair by the window, his head drooping, eyes half-closed. His body seemed to have shrunk over the past few weeks, as if he were folding in on himself. He had once been so sturdy, his hands strong and steady as he worked long hours to build their life together. She could remember those hands holding hers in their first home, dancing with her in the kitchen, his laugh warm and deep. Now, those same hands lay limp in his lap, fingers thin and bony, barely able to lift a spoon.

The doctor had warned her. "Malnutrition," he'd called it, advising her to make sure Arthur ate as much as possible. But he had said it in a detached, clinical way, as if simply commanding food to appear would make it so. "Make sure he eats regularly, Mrs. McCarthy," he'd said, his voice soft but void of empathy. She'd nodded, though the question had burned inside her: *What food? How do I feed him when there's nothing left?*

That night, Martha moved around the kitchen slowly, pulling together what little she had left: a can of beans, a single shriveled potato, and the last slice of bread. She sliced the potato into thin, fragile pieces, arranging them on the plate with the care of someone setting out a feast. She spread a thin layer of jam over the stale bread and placed it beside the beans, making the meal look as full as she could, hoping he wouldn't notice.

When she brought the plate over to him, she forced a smile, though she could feel her face trembling with the effort.

"Here we go, sweetheart," she murmured, setting the plate in front of him, her voice as soft as it had been fifty years ago, when they were newlyweds. "Dinner's ready."

Arthur blinked up at her, his gaze foggy, his eyes darting from her face to the plate, confusion settling over his features. His hand reached for hers, the fingers cold and unsteady.

"Martha… is this… is this all we got?" he asked, his voice thin, almost a whisper.

She felt a sharp sting in her chest, a mixture of shame and heartbreak she couldn't push down. She forced herself to nod, resting a hand on his shoulder, feeling the sharpness of his bones through his shirt. "Just for now, love. Just… just for now."

He nodded, a quiet understanding in his eyes, but she could see the disappointment, the ache of hunger, and that deeper, unspoken question they both carried: *When did it all come to this?*

They ate in silence, the clinking of forks against plates the only sound in the room. She watched him chew, each bite a visible effort, his hands trembling as he lifted the fork. She stared down at her own plate, at the small scoop of beans and single potato slice, and swallowed it in small bites, telling herself she wasn't hungry, telling herself this was enough.

But the hollowness in her stomach only grew sharper, an ache she knew would never be filled.

That night, as they lay side by side in bed, Martha listened to Arthur's shallow breathing, each rise and fall of his chest a quiet reassurance. The darkness around them felt like a weight, pressing down on her, her eyes wide open, fixed on the ceiling, her mind lost in memories she couldn't escape.

She remembered their early years—the house they'd worked so hard to buy, the Sunday dinners that filled every room with the smell of roasted chicken, fresh bread, and apple pie. She remembered Arthur's strong arms wrapped around her as they danced in the kitchen, laughing to songs only they knew. He'd been so alive, so full of love, the warmth of his hands a constant comfort.

But now, those hands were cold, and she felt like she was watching him slip away, piece by piece. She'd become his nurse, his caretaker, the last line of defense against a world that no longer seemed to care. The pain of hunger gnawed at her, sharp and insistent, but she ignored it, forcing herself to stay quiet, listening to his breathing, the only sound in the room that still felt real.

In the morning, she walked to the corner store, clutching the last few dollars she had. She felt the eyes of her neighbors on her, glances that flicked her way and then quickly turned, as if she were something fragile, something uncomfortable. She could hear the whispers in her mind—*How did they end up like this?*

Inside the store, she moved down the aisles slowly, her eyes scanning each price tag, feeling the weight of every choice. A loaf of bread, a tin of soup, a bag of rice. She picked up a can of beans, holding it in her hands, the metal cold against her fingers, and let herself imagine a full pantry, the shelves lined with food, Arthur smiling at her from across the room. But the image slipped away as quickly as it had come.

At the counter, she placed her meager selection in front of the cashier, a young woman with tired eyes who looked at her with something close to pity.

"Thank you, Mrs. McCarthy," the cashier murmured, her voice gentle, though Martha could feel the words like a weight pressing down on her. She nodded, taking the bag, the smallness of it heavy in her hands.

As she left the store, she clutched the bag to her chest, feeling the hollow ache of shame and helplessness. Once, she'd been able to bring home enough to fill their table, to make Arthur smile, to make him proud. Now, she could barely keep him alive.

That evening, she poured half the soup into a bowl for Arthur, setting it carefully in front of him. She sat across from him, her own bowl empty, her hands folded tightly in her lap. She watched as he tried to lift the spoon to his mouth, his hand trembling, soup spilling over the edge, his face tight with concentration.

"Aren't you… going to eat, Martha?" he asked, his voice full of concern, the man who had always taken care of her still trying to hold onto that piece of himself.

She forced a smile, reaching across the table to take his hand, feeling the thinness of his fingers, the fragility of his bones. "I'm not hungry, love," she whispered, her voice catching. "You… you need it more."

Arthur looked at her, his eyes soft, as if he knew, as if he could see the lie for what it was. But he didn't say anything, just nodded slowly before taking another shaky spoonful, his gaze drifting to the empty bowl in front of her.

In the quiet of the night, Martha lay awake, feeling the ache in her stomach deepen. She thought of their children, all living states away, unaware of how things had fallen apart, of how much she had lost. She thought of the retirement they had saved for, whittled down by medical bills and the relentless cost of living, slipping away like sand through her fingers.

Arthur stirred beside her, reaching for her hand. She clasped it tightly, her fingers curling around his, feeling the coldness seep through her skin. She watched him, his eyes half-open, a faint smile on his lips.

"Martha… do you remember when we used to sit out on the porch? Those warm summer nights…" His voice trailed off, a wistful echo.

She nodded, her eyes filling with tears she refused to let fall. "I remember, Arthur. I remember everything."

"Good," he murmured, his eyes drifting closed. "Hold onto that for me, will you?"

"I will," she whispered, her voice breaking.

She stayed by his side, her hand in his, holding onto what little warmth remained, feeling each faint heartbeat slipping further from her grasp. She squeezed his fingers, as if the strength of her own will could anchor him, could tether him to a world that no longer had room for them. The darkness around them was silent, vast, pressing in like a slow tide that would not recede. She understood, with a hollow ache, that they were alone in a way she had never imagined possible. There would be no help, no miracle, no hand reaching out to catch them in their quiet fall.

The life they had built, the love they had shared, all the years of sacrifices and struggles—it felt so fragile now, like a thread worn thin and fraying in the dark. She wanted to whisper words of comfort, to reassure him that they would find a way, that better days would come. But she knew it was a lie. The world outside had already moved on, leaving them as relics of a promise that had never been kept.

As she held him, she felt something inside her begin to unravel—a part of herself that had fought, had endured, slowly giving way. And in the stillness of that room, as she listened to the quiet, fading rhythm of his breaths, she understood that they would slip away together, two souls bound by love and loss, disappearing like shadows into the night.

FOUR

The classroom was a storm of noise. Laura held Jake's hand as they walked in, his fingers clenching hers tightly. He was already overwhelmed—she could feel his small body stiffening, his breathing quickening as he took in the voices bouncing off the walls, the flickering lights overhead, the children running from desk to desk. She knew every sound, every sudden movement was hitting him like a thousand tiny needles, and her heart sank.

"Mrs. Young?" The teacher's voice barely rose above the chaos. She looked at Laura and Jake with a thin, tired smile that didn't quite reach her eyes. "Come on in. Just… find any seat," she said, waving them in with a resigned sigh.

Laura felt the chill of dread settle in her stomach. *Any seat* meant there was no designated space, no place for Jake where he could find even a sliver of calm in this overwhelming sea. She knelt down beside him, brushing her hand gently over his cheek, but he wouldn't meet her eyes. His gaze darted from one corner of the room to the other, his body tensing as he took it all in.

"It'll be okay, Jake," she murmured, even as her heart broke. She was holding his hands, but she could already feel his grip tightening, his fingers beginning to twitch, his body pulling away as his mind retreated.

"Mommy has to go to work, but I'll be back soon," she whispered, her own voice catching. *You'll be okay. You're so brave.* But his eyes wouldn't meet hers, his gaze fixed somewhere beyond her, his small face blank with a fear he couldn't put into words.

He clung to her, and she wanted nothing more than to scoop him up and run, to carry him home and shield him from the world that overwhelmed him so completely. But she couldn't. She had to leave—she had rent due, school fees to cover, and two jobs just to make it all work. She felt his small hands lock onto her arm, his body pressing into hers in a silent, desperate plea she couldn't answer.

"Come on, Jake," she whispered, gently prying his fingers away. Her lips brushed his forehead, her throat tight as she said, "Mommy loves you." The words felt empty, like an apology she had no way of making right.

She forced herself to turn and walk out, each step a wrenching ache as she left him behind. She could hear his quiet, guttural cry echoing down the hall, following her as she left the building, her own vision blurred with tears.

Over the next few weeks, Laura watched as Jake's world began to slip away. His progress, every tiny, hard-won milestone he'd reached, was unraveling before her eyes. The letters he'd learned to trace were becoming lost to him; his hand fumbled with a spoon he had once learned to hold with pride. His small steps forward were falling away, each day a reminder of how hard he'd fought, how much he was losing.

Each morning, he clung to her at the door, his face blank but his grip fierce, his eyes wide with the confusion he couldn't express. She wanted to be there with him, to soothe him, to stay beside him. But staying with him wasn't an option. Her hours were already stretched thin, each shift an essential piece of their fragile life. She worked through the night to cover his school fees, skipping sleep, cutting every corner to keep him in a place that seemed to be leaving him behind.

One afternoon, after a particularly rough day, she met with the teacher, her face already tight with exhaustion. "He's slipping," Laura said, her voice a low plea. "He needs more help. He's losing all the things we worked so hard to get him to. He's slipping, and I can't… I can't do this on my own."

The teacher looked at her, her gaze softening with a kind of pity that made Laura's stomach twist. "Mrs. Young, we're doing everything we can," she said, a practiced sympathy in her tone. "With the new restructuring, we just don't have the same resources we used to. He's… well, he's not the only child in need."

"But he's my son," Laura whispered, a flash of frustration breaking through her exhaustion. "I'm paying for a program that's supposed to help him, but he's barely holding on."

The teacher's expression flickered, but she looked away. "I know it's hard, Mrs. Young. Our hands are tied."

Laura felt the sting of tears in her eyes, but she held them back. Jake wasn't a problem to be managed or a line item in a budget. He was a little boy who loved animals, who laughed when he heard music, who had dreams that couldn't find their way out. But to them, he was an expense—a figure in the long list of costs they couldn't justify.

One night, after another shift where every dollar felt like a lifeline, she found Jake in the corner of his room, his knees pulled up to his chest, rocking slowly, his gaze locked on a point somewhere beyond her. She knelt beside him, reaching out to stroke his hair, her hand gentle and trembling.

"Jake, honey," she whispered, her voice soft but pleading. "Can you look at Mommy?"

But he didn't move, didn't shift his gaze. His small frame rocked back and forth, his fingers clutching at the fabric of his shirt. She could see the quiet desperation in his face, a fear he couldn't express, a world slipping from his grasp. He was retreating, slipping further away, disappearing into the silence that had once been his prison and was now becoming his home again.

She wrapped her arms around him, her heart breaking as she whispered, "I'm here, baby. I'm right here." But she knew, with a heaviness she could barely bear, that her presence wasn't enough. She could work every hour, plead with every teacher, sit through every meeting, but she was losing him, and there was nothing she could do to stop it.

The call came a few days later: she was needed at the school for a meeting. She sat stiffly across from the principal, Jake by her side, his small hands twisting in his lap, his gaze fixed on the floor. She felt the weight of the principal's words before he even spoke, his voice carrying the impersonal authority of a decision already made.

"Mrs. Young, we need to talk about Jake's behavior," he began, his voice careful. "His outbursts are becoming… disruptive. The other parents are concerned, and the teachers feel they can't manage him without additional resources."

She felt her stomach twist, her hands tightening in her lap. She'd sensed this coming—the way people stared when he struggled, the whispers of other parents, the side glances from teachers. But hearing it said aloud felt like a blow, knocking the breath from her lungs.

"What are you saying?" she managed, her voice thin, barely steady.

The principal sighed, adjusting the papers in front of him. "We're doing what we can, but without additional staff, it's difficult to meet Jake's needs. His behavior is… well, it's becoming a concern. If things don't improve, we may have to ask you to find other arrangements."

Her heart pounded, her mind racing as she struggled to process his words. "You mean… you're going to expel him?" The word felt foreign, impossible.

He looked at her with pity, but his voice was steady, unyielding. "We have to consider the well-being of all our students, Mrs. Young. I'm sorry."

She sat there, her body numb, her mind reeling with the weight of his words. She looked at Jake, sitting quietly beside her, oblivious to the decision being made about his future, his small hands clutching the edge of his chair, his face blank.

"But I can't stay home with him," she whispered, her voice breaking. "I can barely keep us afloat as it is. I'm doing everything I can. Doesn't that mean anything?"

The principal's gaze softened, but there was no room for compassion in his answer. "I'm truly sorry, Mrs. Young. But without the resources, it's just not possible."

She left the meeting in a daze, Jake holding her hand, his small, trusting gaze fixed on her, unaware of the battle she was losing.

That night, after another quiet dinner and a bedtime story read through trembling lips, Laura tucked Jake into bed, her hand resting on his forehead, her fingers lingering as she whispered, "You're so brave, my sweet boy. You are stronger than anyone knows."

He didn't respond, his gaze drifting somewhere she couldn't follow, but he reached up, his small hand resting on her cheek. She could feel the warmth of his touch, the innocence and love in his silent gesture, and her heart shattered beneath the weight of it.

As he drifted to sleep, she sat beside him, her hands shaking as she pressed them to her mouth, her shoulders wracked with silent sobs. She was losing him—her bright, beautiful boy, slipping away into a world that no longer had room for him, a silence that grew deeper with each passing day.

In the quiet of the room, Laura sat beside Jake, her hand resting gently on his chest, feeling the soft rise and fall of his breaths. She watched him sleep, his face peaceful in the dark, unaware of the battles waging around him, of the world that had quietly turned its back. She traced the delicate curve of his cheek with her fingertips, her heart swelling with a love so fierce it was almost painful, a love that left her hollow and aching, with nowhere to turn.

As the weight of it all settled over her, she felt something inside her give way—a fragile, invisible thread that had held her together for so long. The exhaustion, the fear, the endless struggle—it washed over her in waves, drowning her in a grief too deep for words. She wanted to scream, to shatter the silence, to make the world see him, to make them understand. But the room held her in its quiet grip, indifferent, leaving her voice unheard and her pain unseen.

She stayed there, feeling the enormity of her helplessness pressing down, her vision blurred by silent, unrelenting tears. She was his mother, but she felt as powerless as a stranger, unable to shield him from the world that seemed determined to erase him. She clung to him as he slept, her arms wrapped around his small frame, as though her embrace alone could hold back the darkness that threatened to swallow them whole.

As dawn began to creep into the room, casting pale light over his sleeping form, she sat alone, hollowed and lost, a mother adrift in a world that had no place for her son. And in that fragile, unforgiving silence, she felt the enormity of her love and her sorrow filling every empty space, stretching into the dark with nowhere left to go.

FIVE

The house felt heavier than ever before, the rooms thick with a silence that was almost unbearable. Linda sat alone at the kitchen table, staring at the empty chair across from her, where her son had once sat, quiet and withdrawn. She could still see him there, his shoulders hunched, eyes downcast, trying to shrink into himself as though he could disappear from the world around him.

Her fingers trembled as she traced the edge of his last school photo, the only tangible reminder she had left. In it, his smile was forced, his eyes holding a hint of sadness she hadn't noticed before. Or maybe she'd noticed, but had brushed it aside, convinced he was simply going through a phase, convinced that her love—though she would never admit it to herself—could "fix" him.

She remembered the bruises, the ones he'd come home with after school. How he'd brush them off, mumbling that he'd "tripped" or that it was just "a game." She hadn't questioned him at first, but as the bruises became more frequent, more pronounced, she couldn't ignore them anymore. She'd asked him one evening, trying to keep her voice steady, but he'd just shrugged, barely looking up.

"Mom, it's fine. Just some guys… messing around."

But she had seen the way his hand trembled, the way his shoulders hunched even further, as if he were shrinking from the very air around him. She had wanted to press him, to ask him who had done this to him, but a part of her already knew. The kids at school. The whispers. The taunts. *The things he had been hiding from her.*

When he'd come out to them a year ago, the house had erupted into chaos. She remembered his voice, barely a whisper, as he told them he was gay, his face tense, bracing for the impact. She'd felt a surge of anger, disappointment, something she hadn't been able to name. She hadn't been able to hold back, her voice rising, her words sharp, laced with a fear she had disguised as anger.

"Do you know what people will say?" she'd shouted, the words tumbling out before she could stop herself. "Do you have any idea what you're bringing on this family? You can't… you can't just choose this."

His face had crumpled, his shoulders sagging, and he'd looked at her with a mix of sorrow and something else, something that had shattered her—acceptance. Acceptance that she wouldn't understand, that she might never understand.

"This isn't a choice, Mom," he'd replied, his voice thick, his eyes glistening. "This is… this is who I am."

But she hadn't listened. She hadn't tried to understand. Her fear had overtaken her, and she had clung to the beliefs she'd held for so long, beliefs that told her he was misguided, that he was wrong. She'd told herself that this was just a phase, that he could be changed, molded, corrected.

Bill had backed her up, his voice echoing through the house as he told their son he would be "better off" if he'd just try to "fit in." He'd told him that people like him didn't belong, that the world would tear him apart if he didn't "fix" himself. The words hung between them, barbed and brutal, each one stripping away another layer of the boy they'd once known.

They'd had talks—talks she wished she could erase, that played on repeat in her mind, tormenting her. The words "correctional camp" had come up too many times, each time she'd said it in that cold, impersonal tone, as if it were a simple solution to a problem she didn't want to understand. She had believed it would help him, that it would show him the "right path," that it would change him.

But it had only driven him further away.

The fights had become frequent, vicious, each one a brutal reminder of the gulf that had opened between them. She remembered the look on his face when she'd told him she was considering sending him to a "therapy" camp, her voice hard and unyielding, as though this were a decision she'd already made. His face had gone pale, his eyes widening in disbelief, and she'd felt a flicker of regret. But she'd shoved it down, telling herself it was for his own good.

"I can't go to one of those places, Mom," he had pleaded, his voice trembling, his hands gripping the edge of the table. *"I've heard stories... what they do to people like me... Please don't do this."*

She'd looked away, unwilling to meet his eyes. She'd been afraid, afraid of losing him, afraid of what people would think. She'd convinced herself that this was the only way to save him, that this was love.

And then there was that last argument, the one that echoed through her mind with a clarity that left her breathless. She could see it all—her son, standing in the hallway, his fists clenched, his face twisted in despair as he shouted, *"I just want you to love me! I don't want to be something you're ashamed of!"*

She had stood there, frozen, her heart pounding, the words lodged in her throat. She had wanted to say it then, wanted to tell him that she loved him, that he was her son, her beautiful boy, no matter what. But the words hadn't come. She had just stood there, silent, watching as he turned and walked away, his shoulders hunched, his spirit crushed.

And then, that morning, the one that would haunt her for the rest of her life, she had opened his door, her voice sharp, annoyed, calling his name. But he hadn't answered. She'd stepped inside, her irritation growing, but then... then she'd seen him.

His body, still, slumped in his chair, his face pale, his eyes closed, as though he were simply asleep. But there was no rise and fall of his chest, no soft breath, no sign of life. She had stood there, her heart racing, her mind unable to comprehend the sight before her. And then, with a scream that tore through the silence, she had rushed to him, her hands trembling, her voice breaking as she called his name, over and over, begging him to wake up, to open his eyes, to come back.

The EMTs had arrived, their voices soft, their hands gentle as they'd lifted him, carried him out of the room, leaving her and Bill alone in the suffocating quiet. They'd sat there for hours, their hands intertwined, their bodies shaking with sobs, their grief too vast, too consuming, to contain.

Now, she sat in that same kitchen, the memories crashing over her like waves, each one a fresh wound, raw and bleeding. She looked across the table at Bill, his face drawn, his eyes hollow, fixed on the last picture they had of their son, his forced smile a painful reminder of everything they'd lost.

"He's gone, Bill," she whispered, her voice trembling. "Our boy... he's gone."

Bill's hands clenched, his jaw tight, his face contorted with a grief too deep to mask. "We… we did this, Linda," he choked out, his voice breaking. "We… we pushed him away. We… we broke him."

She nodded, her throat tight, her heart splintering into a thousand pieces. "I thought… I thought I was protecting him," she murmured, her voice barely a whisper. "I thought… I thought he could change."

They sat in silence, each lost in the memories of every fight, every harsh word, every look of disappointment that had passed between them and the son they had loved but had never truly accepted. They had believed they were doing the right thing, that they were protecting him, guiding him. But all they had done was build a prison around him, one that had slowly, steadily crushed the life out of him.

She looked down at the note he'd left, the words scrawled in a shaky hand, a final plea, a last goodbye. *"I tried to be what you wanted. I really did. But I can't… I can't pretend anymore."*

The words tore into her, each one a knife twisting in her chest, a brutal reminder of everything they had taken from him. She had thought she was showing him love, guiding him down a path she believed was right. But now, in the suffocating silence of their empty home, she could see the truth—their beliefs, their choices, their silence had killed him, had driven him to a place of despair so deep, so dark, that he had seen no other way out.

Linda looked at Bill, her voice a broken whisper. "What… what do we do now?"

But Bill only shook his head, his face crumpling as he reached for her hand, their fingers intertwining, both of them clinging to each other, each of them lost in the vast, consuming emptiness of their grief. They had loved their son, but they had also destroyed him, stripped him of the hope, the love, the acceptance he had so desperately needed.

And now, they were left with nothing but the echoes of his laughter, the memory of his smile.

SIX

The car was cold, the night air settling inside like an unwelcome guest, cutting through the thin metal and seeping into every corner. Daniel sat huddled in the back seat with his daughters, their tiny bodies pressed against him, their breaths soft and warm against his chest. He pulled the worn blanket tighter around them, wrapping his arms around Maya and Sophie as they drifted in and out of sleep, their small hands gripping his jacket, their faces pale and innocent.

Maya shifted closer, her cheek resting against his chest, her fingers clutching his shirt as though even in sleep, she needed reassurance that he was still there. Sophie lay curled up on his other side, her little body tense, her fingers clutching his sleeve with quiet desperation, as if she were holding onto him with everything she had.

He looked down at them, his heart aching with a love so fierce it felt like it might break him. They were everything to him, the only light in a world that had grown colder, darker, and more indifferent with every passing day. They were supposed to be safe. They were supposed to have a home, a warm bed, a life filled with love, laughter, and the security he'd promised to give them. He had vowed to protect them, to keep them safe, no matter what.

Ashley had made him promise. In the hospital, her voice weak, her hand trembling in his, she had looked at him with those bright, unwavering eyes, even as her body gave out. "Take care of them, Daniel," she had whispered, her words soft, fading with each breath. "Give them everything… promise me." He had nodded, his voice thick with emotion, as he whispered, "I promise, Ash. I'll give them everything."

He had meant it. He had clung to that promise, to the memory of her last words, her last breath, believing that somehow, the love he had for them would be enough to carry them through anything.

For a while, he had managed. He had juggled work, daycare, nights spent reading bedtime stories and mornings making breakfast. He had kept the small apartment they'd called home, filling it with warmth and stability, doing everything he could to make up for Ashley's absence. It hadn't been much, but it had been enough. They'd had food, shelter, and each other. The low-income housing assistance had helped cover their rent, allowing him to keep the job that kept them afloat, to afford daycare and a few small luxuries—like Maya's favorite stuffed animal, or Sophie's book of bedtime stories.

Then, out of nowhere, the letter had come. Cold, impersonal, stamped with a government seal that seemed to mock him. *Due to recent budget cuts, your housing assistance has been terminated.* He remembered staring at those words, feeling the ground slip out from under him, his mind racing as he tried to process the weight of it. He'd read the letter over and over, his hands shaking, the words blurring as the reality sank in.

He had tried to fight it. He'd spent hours on the phone, pleading with faceless voices, asking for extensions, for exceptions, for anything that might keep them in their home. But each call ended the same way—with an indifferent apology and the cold, clinical response that there was "nothing we can do."

The eviction notice had come swiftly after, a final blow that left him reeling. He'd packed up their lives that night, stuffing toys and clothes into garbage bags, shoving everything they owned into the back seat of the car as his daughters watched, their eyes wide, their voices soft with questions he couldn't answer. He could still see their faces, still hear the tremble in Maya's voice as she'd asked, "Daddy, why can't we go home?"

He hadn't known what to tell her. He'd just hugged them tight, whispering, "It's only for a little while, honey. We'll find somewhere soon. Somewhere warm and safe. Just hold on."

The car had become their refuge, their last shelter in a world that had turned its back on them. Every day, he picked up gig work—deliveries, late-night shifts, anything that would put money in his pocket, however small. He'd drive for hours with his daughters in the back seat, their wide eyes watching as the city drifted by, as each day bled into the next in an endless blur of parking lots, street corners, and cramped spaces that served as their home.

But tonight felt different. The air was colder, sharper, biting into his skin even through his jacket, and he could feel the weight of his exhaustion settling into his bones, pressing down on him like an invisible force. He held his daughters close, his heart aching with a fear he couldn't shake, a feeling that everything was slipping, that he was losing his grip on the promises he'd made.

Then, just as he turned the key in the ignition to start the car, it happened—the car shuddered, a low, ominous groan that seemed to vibrate through the entire frame. The dashboard lights flickered, the engine sputtered, and then everything went silent.

"No… no, no, no…" he whispered, his voice tight with panic as he turned the key again, praying it was just a minor glitch, something he could fix. But the engine remained silent, unresponsive, the last bit of life drained away.

He climbed out, his hands shaking as he opened the hood, hoping against hope that he'd find something he could fix, something that would get them through one more night. But as he stared at the engine, his heart sank. The head gasket was blown, beyond repair. The smell of burnt coolant filled the air, a bitter scent that sealed his fate.

He stumbled back, his hands gripping the edge of the hood, his mind reeling as the reality of it sank in. The car had been everything—their home, their last bit of safety, the one thing he could still give them. Without it, they had nothing. He had nothing.

The weight of it all crashed down on him, the months of scraping by, of holding on with nothing but sheer will, of every scraped-together meal, every sleepless night, every moment he'd spent pretending things would get better. It was too much. He could feel something inside him break, a dam bursting, releasing a flood of grief and rage and helplessness he had kept locked away.

He fell to his knees in front of the car, his hands clutching at his hair as a scream tore from his throat, raw and guttural, a sound that echoed into the empty night, a release of everything he had buried, everything he could no longer hold back. He screamed again, louder, his fists slamming against the cold metal, his body shaking as he let himself feel every ounce of pain, every bit of fear and frustration he had hidden from his daughters.

He thought of Ashley, of the promise he had made to her, of the life he had tried so hard to give their daughters. He had held her hand, had vowed to protect them, to keep them safe, to give them everything she had dreamed of. But he had failed. He had lost everything.

The tears came harder, blurring his vision, staining his cheeks as he sobbed into the darkness, his heart breaking under the weight of promises unkept. He was just a man, broken and beaten down, a father who had tried so hard and had still lost, reduced to nothing but the hollow ache of love and loss.

"Why?" he choked out, his voice barely more than a whisper, a plea into the empty night. "Why can't I… just give them one good thing? Why can't I… why can't I be enough?"

The tears flowed freely now, his body wracked with sobs, his chest heaving as he knelt there, alone, feeling the weight of his helplessness pressing down on him, crushing him.

"Daddy?"

The voice was soft, a gentle whisper that pulled him back from the edge. He looked up, blinking through his tears, to see Maya and Sophie standing there, their small faces pale, their eyes wide with worry.

Maya stepped forward, wrapping her tiny arms around his neck, pressing her cheek against his. "It's okay, Daddy," she whispered, her voice filled with a love that pierced through his despair, that reminded him of the one thing he still had. "We're here. We'll stay together."

Sophie moved beside him, her small hand resting on his shoulder, her touch grounding him, reminding him of the love that had held him together through every storm. He held them both, his arms wrapped around their small bodies, his heart breaking under the weight of their trust, their love. For them, he would keep going. For them, he would find a way, no matter how impossible it felt.

Eventually, he coaxed his daughters back into the car, his hands steadying them as they climbed inside, though his own legs felt weak, barely able to hold him up. He tucked them into the back seat, draping the thin, threadbare blanket over their shoulders, wrapping it tightly around them as though he could somehow keep out the cold that seeped in from every corner.

Maya looked up at him, her eyes wide, tired, but filled with trust so pure it cut him deeper than any blade. She lifted a hand, brushing it against his cheek, the touch so soft, so small, it nearly undid him. "Daddy," she whispered, her voice barely a murmur in the quiet, "are we going to be okay?"

Her question hung in the air, piercing through the silence, a plea he could feel wrapping around his heart, tightening with each breath. He forced himself to smile, though he felt like he was unraveling, his insides hollow, his soul fraying at the edges. His voice came out soft, trembling, as he stroked her cheek with a tenderness that he hoped would make up for everything he couldn't give her. "Yes, sweetheart," he murmured, his voice thick with emotion he could barely contain. "We're going to be okay."

Even as he said it, the lie scraped against him, raw and brutal, because he had no idea what tomorrow would bring. He didn't know where they'd go or how they'd survive without the car. He felt like a man stranded at sea, clinging to driftwood in a vast, endless ocean, promising safety when he couldn't even see the shore.

She nodded, content with his answer, her small hand slipping back under the blanket, her head resting on his arm. He watched as her eyelids drooped, her breaths evening out, her body slipping back into sleep with a trust that shattered him. Sophie was already curled up beside her, her face peaceful, her hand resting gently against his sleeve as if even in sleep, she reached for him.

Daniel leaned back, exhaling a breath he hadn't realized he'd been holding, his gaze drifting to the window, where the night pressed in, dark and heavy, a vast emptiness that seemed to swallow them whole. He could feel the weight of everything he carried—the broken promises, the dreams that had been ripped from them, the life he'd tried to build, now reduced to a cold car on the side of an empty road.

As he looked out into the darkness, he felt himself slipping, the despair creeping in, an ache so deep it felt like it was hollowing him out from the inside. He wanted to believe the words he'd spoken to Maya, wanted to believe that they'd be okay, that he'd somehow find a way to keep them safe, to give them the life he had promised Ashley. But the truth loomed large and unyielding, an ever-present reminder of how little he had left, of how quickly everything could be taken away.

He brushed a hand over their foreheads, his fingers lingering, tracing the curve of their cheeks, feeling the softness of their skin, the innocence he had sworn to protect. And in that moment, he felt the enormity of his love for them, a love so fierce it felt like it might tear him apart. He wanted to shield them from every hurt, every cold night, every moment of fear. He wanted to give them the life he had promised Ashley, a life filled with warmth, with security, with the unshakable certainty that they were safe.

But he didn't know how. He didn't know if he had anything left to give, if he could keep going, keep pretending that everything would be okay when every step felt like a descent into darkness.

As the dawn broke, casting a pale light over their sleeping faces, he felt a single tear slip down his cheek, silent and unbidden, a testament to the love he carried, a love that was fierce enough to keep him going, even when he had nothing else. He held them close, his heart breaking as he clung to the one thing he still had, the one thing that made him whole—the love he carried for them, a love that was all he had left.

SEVEN

The waiting room was cold, sterile, with walls painted a sickly beige that seemed to sap the color out of everything. Carlos sat on the metal bench, his fingers tightly interlaced, knuckles white, as he stared at the wall across from him. His two children, Mateo and Sofia, sat beside him, their small bodies pressed close to his sides, eyes wide with fear, as if they could sense the silent storm brewing around them. Their breaths were shallow, tiny gasps that seemed to echo in the heavy silence.

They were only children—his children. Children who had known nothing but the warmth of their mother's arms, the softness of their neighborhood, the light streaming in from their bedroom windows. They were American children, born here, raised here, as much a part of this country as the streets they walked and the playgrounds they had run across. Yet here they were, tucked into the corner of a soulless waiting room, waiting to be processed like numbers, like problems waiting to be solved.

Sofia shifted, leaning into him, her tiny hand gripping his arm with a desperation that tore at his heart. Her eyes were wide, dark, filled with a fear she couldn't put into words. Mateo sat beside her, his head low, lips pressed tight as he stared at the floor, his small fists clenched in his lap, his body taut with tension. They were too young to understand what was happening, too young to know the cruelty of a system that had turned them from citizens into suspects, from children into detainees.

Carlos felt his own heart beating wildly, felt his own chest tighten as he glanced down at them, his children—his life, his reason for every step he had taken since crossing into this country all those years ago. He had come here with nothing but hope, a fierce determination to build a life for himself and his family, to give his children a future that was bright, that was filled with possibility. He had worked, he had sacrificed, he had done everything right. He had believed in the promise of America, in the dream that had kept him going through every long night and every weary day.

But now, that dream had turned into a nightmare, a dark, suffocating reality that threatened to tear his family apart, to rip his children from the only life they had ever known.

"Papi," Sofia whispered, her voice trembling, barely more than a breath. "Are… are they going to take us away?"

Her words cut through him, sharp and unrelenting, each syllable a wound that sliced deeper into his heart. He wanted to tell her no, to hold her tight and promise that he would keep her safe, that no one could take her away from him. But he couldn't bring himself to say it. The words caught in his throat, choked by the bitter reality that had wrapped itself around him like a vise.

He looked down at her, his hand moving to brush a stray strand of hair from her face, his fingers lingering on her cheek, tracing the softness of her skin, memorizing the feel of her, as though he were already losing her. "No matter what happens, mija," he said, his voice thick, broken, "I'm here. I'm with you. Don't be afraid."

But he could see the fear in her eyes, could see the way she clung to him, her small body pressed so close he could feel the faint rhythm of her heartbeat against his side. She was too young, too innocent to understand the words he didn't say, the words he couldn't bring himself to admit. He was her father—her protector, her guide. But he had no power here. No control over the cold, indifferent system that had brought them to this place, that had stripped him of his rights, his dignity, his hope.

Mateo looked up, his dark eyes filled with questions, with anger, with a hurt that Carlos didn't know how to heal. "Papi," he whispered, his voice wavering, "why… why are they doing this to us?"

Carlos felt his own heart break a little more, felt the weight of his own helplessness pressing down on him, suffocating him. How could he explain it to them? How could he tell them that they were here not because of anything they had done, but because of the way they looked, because of the blood that ran through their veins, because of a line on a map they had never even seen? How could he tell them that they were being punished for something as simple, as unchangeable, as the place of their birth?

"I don't know," he whispered, his voice raw, barely audible. "I don't know why."

But he knew. He knew that in the eyes of the system, they were nothing more than numbers, cases to be processed, lives to be sorted and discarded. He knew that here, in this cold, unfeeling place, his love for his children, his devotion, his sacrifice—it all meant nothing. They were nothing but faces in a file, names on a list, stripped of everything that made them human.

The door creaked open, and a man in a stiff uniform stepped into the room, his gaze cold, clinical, as he scanned the small group of people huddled on the benches. He called out a name, a name that sounded foreign, unfamiliar, yet Carlos recognized it instantly—the name they had assigned to him, a number masquerading as an identity. He stood, his legs trembling, his heart pounding, as he took Sofia and Mateo's hands, guiding them forward, his grip tight, fierce, as though he could shield them from what was to come.

They were led down a narrow hallway, the walls lined with metal doors, each one closed, each one concealing a life, a story, a family just like his own. He could hear the sounds of muffled cries, of whispered prayers, of voices filled with a desperation that matched his own. Each step felt heavier than the last, each footfall a reminder of the helplessness that had wrapped itself around him, that had taken root in his heart.

As they walked, he couldn't help but think of Rosa, his wife, the woman he had loved with every beat of his heart. She was an American citizen, born and raised in this very country, yet here they were, being torn apart by a system that viewed her love, her family, as a crime. She was being held in a separate facility, facing charges of "aiding and abetting" him, her own husband, their own children— because she had dared to love him, dared to build a life with him. He hadn't seen her in weeks, hadn't heard her voice, hadn't been able to reassure her, to tell her he loved her, that he was still fighting.

They reached a small, dimly lit room, where a metal table stood in the center, surrounded by chairs bolted to the floor. The man gestured for them to sit, his gaze indifferent, his voice monotone as he began to ask questions, questions that felt invasive, cruel, questions that chipped away at the last remnants of Carlos's dignity.

"Do you understand why you're here?" the man asked, his tone sharp, condescending, as though Carlos were nothing more than a problem to be solved, a nuisance to be dealt with.

Carlos swallowed, his throat tight, his voice barely a whisper as he answered. "We've done nothing wrong. My children… they were born here. They're American."

The man's gaze hardened, his lips curling in a faint sneer. "That doesn't change anything. You're all here because you're a threat to this country. You don't belong here."

The words struck him like a blow, each one a reminder of the truth he had tried so hard to deny. He looked down at his children, at their wide, terrified eyes, and felt a surge of rage, of desperation, of a love so fierce it threatened to consume him.

He wanted to scream, to tell this man that he was wrong, that his children were as much a part of this country as anyone else, that they belonged here, that they had a right to be here. But the words caught in his throat, choked by the reality of the system that had brought them to this place, that had stripped them of their humanity, their identity, their right to belong.

Hours passed, each one stretching out like an eternity, as they were shuffled from room to room, each one colder, more impersonal than the last. Sofia clung to his arm, her fingers digging into his skin, her breaths shallow, each one a quiet sob that tore at his heart. Mateo walked beside him, silent, his gaze fixed on the floor, his small fists clenched, his body tense with a fear he tried so hard to hide.

Carlos felt his own strength slipping, felt the weight of his own helplessness pressing down on him, suffocating him. He was their father, their protector, but here, in this place, he was nothing. He was a shadow, a ghost, a man stripped of everything that made him whole.

Finally, they were led into a holding cell, a small, cramped space with metal benches bolted to the walls, the air thick with the scent of sweat and fear. Carlos sat down, pulling his children close, their small bodies pressed against his, their breaths warm, comforting, as he held them, as he tried to shield them from the cold, unfeeling world around them.

He could feel Sofia trembling, could feel the way she clung to him, her small hands gripping his shirt, her face buried in his chest as she whispered, "Papi… I'm scared."

He held her tighter, his heart breaking as he whispered back, "I know, mija. I know."

Mateo looked up at him, his dark eyes filled with questions, with a hurt that Carlos didn't know how to heal. "Papi," he whispered, his voice trembling, "are we ever going to go home?"

Carlos felt his own heart break a little more, felt the weight of his own helplessness pressing down on him, suffocating him. He wanted to tell them yes, wanted to promise them that they would be safe, that they would be together, that nothing could tear them apart. But he couldn't bring himself to say it. The words caught in his throat, choked by the bitter reality that had wrapped itself around him.

He looked down at them, his children, his life, his everything, and felt a tear slip down his cheek, silent, unbidden, a testament to the love he carried, a love that was fierce, unyielding, even in the face of a system that sought to tear them apart.

And then the door opened.

Two officers stepped inside, their faces impassive, their eyes hard as they looked down at him, their gaze shifting to his children. One of them gestured toward Sofia and Mateo, his voice flat, detached. "The children will be transferred to another facility."

"No," Carlos whispered, his voice raw, his hands tightening around his children. "Please… don't take them. They're just kids. Please."

The officers stepped forward, their hands reaching out to separate him from his children. Sofia screamed, her small voice piercing, desperate as she clung to him, her arms wrapped tightly around his neck. "Papi! No, don't let them take us! Don't let them take us!"

Carlos felt his own heart shatter, felt the rage, the desperation, the helplessness rise up inside him, a storm of emotion that left him breathless, broken. "Please," he begged, his voice cracking, his hands clutching his children, his body shaking. "Please, they're all I have. Don't take them… don't take my children."

But the officers were unmoved. They pried Sofia from his arms, her screams echoing in the small cell, her fingers slipping from his grasp as she reached out for him, her face twisted in terror, her voice hoarse as she called out, "Papi! Papi, don't let them—"

Mateo fought, his small fists pounding against the officers, his voice a broken, desperate cry as he was pulled away, his hands reaching out, his eyes wide, pleading. "Papi! Please, Papi!"

Carlos lunged forward, his arms outstretched, his heart pounding, his voice a scream of pure agony as he tried to reach them, as he tried to hold onto them. But an officer stepped in front of him, his expression cold, detached, as he raised the butt of his rifle and brought it down, hard, against Carlos's temple.

Pain exploded through his skull, a blinding, searing pain that left him gasping, his vision blurring, darkening. He could feel himself slipping, could feel the world fading around him, could hear his children's screams, faint, distant, as though they were already slipping away from him, as though they were already lost.

He reached out, his hand grasping at empty air, his fingers stretching, desperate, as he felt himself falling, as he felt his last shred of hope slipping away, as he whispered, his voice barely a breath, "I'm here… I'm here…"

And then, there was nothing. Only darkness.

EIGHT

Jack tossed his keys onto the counter, his hands trembling as he fished his latest paycheck out of his pocket and laid it next to the stack of bills. The numbers were brutal, the column of totals a mockery of the hours he'd put in at the factory that week. He ran his hands over his face, the callouses rough against his skin, feeling every inch of exhaustion deep in his bones.

Karen was sitting at the table, her head down, flipping through the bills with a quiet desperation that made his stomach twist. She didn't even look up when he came in, just slid the electric bill across the table toward him. It was printed in bright red, *Final Notice* stamped across the top in bold, unforgiving letters. She added another envelope—medical bills from when their youngest, Danny, had been sick with a bad flu last winter. They still hadn't paid them off, and interest had piled on top of interest, each month making it harder to catch up.

"Jack, we're going under," she said quietly, looking up with tired, pleading eyes. "We're getting another cut-off notice next week if we don't pay something. And Danny's got a field trip next week that we have to pay for, too. I told him we'd try, but…"

Jack clenched his fists, his face flushing with anger and shame. *This isn't how it was supposed to be.* He had done everything right, followed all the rules, voted the way a man should vote, kept his head down and his hands busy. He had done it for his family, so they could stand on their own two feet without "handouts" or "charity." That was what he'd been told they needed to do, what those politicians on the screen had promised would lift them up. They'd all cheered, clapping as he'd joined the call to dismantle the union, to be "independent."

But now he was staring at a stack of bills he couldn't pay, the burden of it pressing down like a weight he couldn't shake. "Karen, they said it would get better. They promised. Less interference, more control. I thought…" He trailed off, the words hollow, the promises he'd believed in slipping away like sand through his fingers.

Karen's face twisted with frustration, a bitterness he hadn't seen in her before. "Jack, when are you going to stop listening to what they told you and start looking at what's happening to us? We've been scraping by for months. Those 'policies' you cheered for are the reason we're here."

He scoffed, his pride bristling at her tone. "Oh, so now it's my fault? You think it's my fault we're barely making it?"

Karen's eyes narrowed, her voice low, fierce. "Yes, Jack. Because you chose this. You voted for them, you cheered for them, you helped them kill the very thing that protected us. That union was the only thing keeping us afloat, and you were so blinded by all that talk of freedom and independence that you helped tear it down. And now we're paying the price."

Jack felt his face flush with anger, his fists clenching as he shot back, "I did it for us. For a better future. So we wouldn't have to rely on anyone else. I thought…" His voice faltered, the words catching in his throat. He wanted to believe it, wanted to cling to that pride, that sense of self-sufficiency he'd held onto for so long. But with every bill, every overdue notice, that belief was slipping away.

Karen's face softened, her voice quiet, laced with an exhaustion that broke his heart. "Look around, Jack. What future? We're drowning, and you're too busy being angry to admit it."

That night, Jack lay awake, staring at the ceiling, his mind churning with frustration, shame, and a bitter anger that had no place to go. He didn't want to believe she was right, didn't want to admit that he'd trusted the wrong people, that he'd been a fool. He'd always been so sure, so certain that he was doing the right thing, standing up for his family, for his country, for the values he'd been raised to believe in. But now he couldn't shake the feeling that he'd been lied to, that he'd been used, that he'd thrown away the very protections that had kept his family safe.

The next morning, he found himself pulling his truck up to a side street a few blocks away from the food pantry, feeling a wave of shame wash over him as he parked. He'd waited until Karen had left for her shift before he'd headed out, the weight of her words still echoing in his mind. He hadn't told her where he was going—partly out of pride, partly because he wasn't ready to admit that she'd been right.

He climbed out of the truck, pulling his cap low over his eyes as he walked toward the line that stretched down the block, a crowd of people waiting for their turn at the pantry. His heart pounded, his face flushed with embarrassment as he took his place at the back, his gaze fixed firmly on the ground. He'd spent years sneering at the idea of "handouts," priding himself on his independence, his ability to provide without relying on anyone. And now here he was, standing in line for food he couldn't afford, surrounded by people he'd once looked down on.

A few spaces ahead of him, he noticed a familiar figure—Rafael, a man he'd seen at the factory, one of the guys he'd barely spoken to, always assuming they had nothing in common. Rafael was standing with his wife and young daughter, holding the little girl's hand as he waited, his shoulders slumped, his face lined with exhaustion. Jack felt a surge of resentment bubble up, an instinctive reaction he couldn't quite suppress. *This is why we're in this mess,* he thought bitterly, the words echoing in his mind. *These people, taking what they don't deserve.*

But as he watched, he saw Rafael glance down at his daughter, saw the way he reached out to smooth her hair, the way he smiled at her, soft and weary, as if she were the only thing holding him together. It was a look Jack recognized—a look he'd seen in his own reflection more times than he cared to admit. And in that moment, something shifted, a small, uncomfortable crack forming in the wall of resentment he'd built up over the years.

Rafael turned, catching Jack's eye, his face lighting up with a flicker of recognition. "Jack, hey," he said quietly, nodding in greeting.

Jack grunted, nodding back, his gaze shifting to the ground, the shame tightening in his chest. "Didn't think I'd see you here," he muttered, the words thick, bitter.

Rafael shrugged, his expression calm, resigned. "Times are hard. We all do what we have to, right?"

Jack felt a surge of anger, his pride prickling, desperate to defend himself, to find some way to justify the choices he'd made. "Yeah, well, maybe if things were different... if people didn't take advantage..." He trailed off, the words feeling hollow, empty, even to him.

Rafael's gaze was steady, a quiet understanding in his eyes. "Jack, you think I wanted this? You think I wanted to be here, standing in line for food? We're all here because the people up there, the ones who told us they'd look out for us—they didn't care about us. They took what they wanted and left us to fend for ourselves."

Jack felt a pang of guilt, a cold, bitter realization settling over him. He'd spent so long blaming the wrong people, so long clinging to the idea that he was different, that he was better. But now, standing in line for food he couldn't afford, he saw the truth—that he was just another pawn in a game he hadn't even realized he was playing.

He glanced at Rafael, his pride cracking, his voice low, barely more than a whisper. "I thought… I thought I was doing the right thing. I thought they were looking out for us."

Rafael gave him a sad smile, his gaze filled with a sorrowful understanding. "They only look out for themselves, Jack. That's what we're learning now. They don't care about you, or me, or anyone else in this line. They never did."

Jack felt his shoulders slump, the weight of his choices pressing down on him, suffocating him. He'd been so sure, so proud, so convinced that he was fighting for something real, something true. But now he saw it for what it was—a betrayal, one he'd walked into with his eyes wide open, too blinded by pride to see the truth.

As the line moved forward, he felt a hollow ache settle in his chest, a regret that burned, sharp and unrelenting. And as he took his place in the line, shoulder to shoulder with the very people he'd once blamed, he realized that he was just another casualty, another man left to pick up the pieces of a broken promise.

83

NINE

Dear Diary,

My name is Jeremy. An older kid here gave me this and said that writing can help bad feelings. His name is Garrett, and he is nice to me.

I don't remember my dad. Mommy said he left when I was little. Sometimes I'd ask where he went, but Mommy didn't like to talk about him. Mostly, she wasn't around much. She was busy. Busy with bottles, and smoke, and her friends. She'd tell me to stay in my room when they came over. Some of them looked at me funny, like they were mad I was there. Some looked at me like they looked at Mommy. That made me feel bad, so I would go in my room and stay real quiet.

I know what school is, but they stopped sending me. I can't run like other kids, and my legs get tired fast. They shake sometimes, and I have to sit down a lot. I'm slow. Some kids would laugh at me if I fell, and my hands don't work right when they're shaking. They'd call me names I didn't like, so I didn't mind not going anymore.

So I stayed home with Mommy. It was okay. Mostly, I'd just play alone or look out the window. I'd watch people go by and wonder what it'd be like to have a mom who was there all the time. Someone who wanted to be around me.

Then one day, some men came to the door. They wore uniforms and talked to Mommy. She cried, her face all red and shiny. She tried to hold me, but they pulled me away and took me to a big white building. They called it a group home. There were lots of beds, but I didn't know where I was supposed to sleep. I picked one at the end and just lay there. It was loud and strange, but I tried not to cry.

After a while, they took me to Ms. Green's house. Ms. Green was nice. She'd tuck me in at night, brush my hair back, and tell me I was safe there. She let me play in the backyard, even when

I couldn't keep up with the other kids. Sometimes my legs would give out, or I'd trip if they got too shaky. Ms. Green didn't mind. She'd just help me up and say, "You're okay." She didn't get mad if my hands dropped things either. She'd just hand them back to me and smile.

Ms. Green didn't get mad about my "fits" either. I don't remember much when I had them, but Ms. Green would sit next to me and hold my hand till I woke up. I thought maybe I'd get to stay with her forever. I thought maybe she'd be my real family.

But one day, Ms. Green came into my room. She looked sad, her eyes all shiny like she was about to cry. She told me, "I'm so sorry, honey, but they're taking you back." She said they didn't have enough money for "kids like me." I didn't know what that meant, but I knew it was bad. Ms. Green hugged me and gave me an old bear that was missing an eye. She said he looked like he belonged with me. I didn't cry. I just held the bear close.

They took me back to the group home, and I watched Ms. Green's house get smaller and smaller through the car window.

The group home smelled weird, like cleaning stuff and old socks. The other kids didn't talk to me. They thought I was strange, called me the "weird kid with fits" and said I walked funny. Sometimes they'd laugh when I had one or whisper to each other. I'd just sit on my bed with my bear, try to pretend I was somewhere else.

Then they sent me to a new house. It was big, with a man and a lady, but they didn't talk to me much. The man told me to stay out of his way, called me "bad luck." I didn't know what that meant, but I learned to stay real quiet around him. He didn't like when I was slow or when my legs gave out. One time, I tripped in the hallway, and he slapped me across the face so hard I hit the wall. My cheek hurt, but I didn't cry. I'd learned not to cry.

One night, I had a fit in my room. When I woke up, my mouth tasted like blood from biting my tongue. The man looked in, saw me on the floor, and just walked away. The next morning, they sent me back to the group home. The man said I was "too much work."

Back at the group home, they put me in a room with two other boys. They didn't talk to me either. They'd watch me sometimes while I slept, say I made weird noises. Sometimes they'd laugh or push me. I'd just hold my bear and try to pretend I was invisible.

Then I went to another lady's house. She didn't like when I knocked things over. One time, I spilled a glass of water, and she got real mad. She grabbed my arm, her nails digging in, and shoved me into my room. Told me to stay put. My arm hurt all night, but I didn't say anything.

Another night, I had a fit. When I woke up, my mouth hurt from biting my tongue. I called out, but nobody came. I just lay there on the floor, holding my bear close. I was cold, but I didn't cry. I waited till morning.

Sometimes there were houses that weren't as bad. They'd leave food out for me and let me sleep when I wanted. I didn't talk much in those houses, didn't hope for anything. I knew I'd end up back at the group home.

The last house I went to was the worst. It was small and smelled like smoke. The man there never smiled. He didn't like me around, said I was "in the way." Sometimes he'd lock me in my room. I'd sit by the window and watch the sun go down, listen to my stomach growl. I didn't make any noise. I didn't want him to be mad.

One time, I tripped in the hall, and he grabbed my arm real hard. He looked at me with that angry face and said, "Why don't they just get rid of you? You're nothing but trouble." I didn't say anything. I just went back to my room and held my bear, trying to be real quiet.

Then they took me back to the group home again. Another "failed placement," they called it. I don't know all the words they use, but I hear things. I heard one worker say they don't have "enough money for kids like him." Said I was "too much trouble." I don't know what that means, but I know it's not good. I know I'm too much.

So now I just stay real quiet. I don't talk, don't ask where I'm going next. I lie in bed at night, holding my bear, staring at the ceiling, waiting for the lights to go out, waiting for everything to get quiet. Sometimes I think about what it'd be like to have a family, one that wouldn't send me back.

But that thought gets smaller and smaller. Now it's mostly just me and the dark, and my bear, and the quiet.

TEN

The bus jolted over every pothole, the rows of buildings along the campus shrinking in the distance. Amara leaned her head against the cold window, feeling the weight of her future shrinking with every mile that carried her further from it. She closed her eyes, remembering the first day she'd set foot on that campus, the smell of fresh-cut grass and new beginnings. She had walked those halls like she belonged there, certain that all her hard work had finally unlocked a life beyond the narrow streets of her hometown.

But the letter that had dropped into her mailbox the week before had changed everything. Its bland, formal language—phrases like "budget restructuring" and "necessary funding adjustments"—felt like a slap in the face. She had read those lines over and over, her hands shaking, until the words blurred on the page. The scholarship that had been her lifeline was gone. Just like that, the funding she'd counted on had evaporated, and the future she'd worked for slipped away like sand through her fingers.

She didn't have the words to explain the shame and helplessness that wrapped around her like a vice as she packed up her dorm. Her professors had been kind, offered looks of sympathy and last words of encouragement, but none of it helped. She was leaving, without a degree, without a plan, carrying only a duffel bag of textbooks she couldn't afford and dreams that had turned to ash.

When the bus pulled into her town, she saw her father waiting at the station, standing beside their old, rust-speckled car. His shoulders were slouched, hands tucked deep in his pockets, and he gave her a tired smile as she approached, the kind that tried to hide disappointment but didn't quite manage it.

"Welcome home," he said softly, the words feeling hollow, more like a resignation than a greeting.

She forced herself to smile back, feeling the weight of her family's sacrifice, of everything they had done to get her to college in the first place. They had given her their best, and now she was returning with empty hands.

They drove back to the store in silence, her father's eyes fixed on the road, his fingers tapping a rhythm on the steering wheel. Amara looked out the window, the town passing by in a blur of familiar but faded colors. The last few years had changed things; shop fronts looked older, businesses she remembered had closed, replaced by more chain stores with signs that gleamed too brightly against the worn bricks. She thought of her family's small store, of the years they had poured into it, and felt a pang of guilt that settled deep in her stomach.

The bell over the door jingled as they stepped inside, the familiar smell of stale coffee and faint cleaner greeting her like an old memory. Her mother looked up from behind the counter, her face brightening for a moment as she took in the sight of her daughter. But it was a tired brightness, one dulled by years of quiet resignation. She stepped out from behind the counter and hugged Amara, her arms wrapped tightly around her.

"Amara, you're home," her mother murmured, her voice thick with relief.

"I'm home, Mama," Amara whispered back, fighting the prick of tears in her eyes. She could feel the desperation in her mother's embrace, a desperation that came not just from missing her, but from knowing why she was back.

Her father moved past them, heading to the back to unload boxes, but not before giving Amara's shoulder a gentle squeeze. He didn't need to say anything—she could see the hurt in his eyes, the unspoken words that hovered between them. They had sacrificed so much to give her a chance, to give her a way out of this life, and now, here she was, back again.

The store looked smaller than she remembered, the shelves cramped and sparse. Prices were much higher now; a loaf of bread was nearly five dollars, a gallon of milk almost six. She'd grown up watching her parents manage every dollar, squeezing every cent to keep things afloat, but this felt different. She could see it in the strain on her mother's face as she restocked, in the way her father's hands shook as he handled the cash register, counting out change with fingers that moved slower than she remembered.

The next day, she helped her father unload boxes from the back. He was quieter than usual, his face creased with lines she hadn't noticed before. As they stacked cans on the shelf, he explained in a low voice about the tariffs that had doubled their costs, the loans they could no longer get since protections for small businesses had been cut. They'd once been able to rely on a steady flow of minority loans, support that had allowed them to keep prices down, to compete against the chain stores that had started popping up around town. But those protections had disappeared, evaporated in the wake of policy shifts her parents barely understood, policies that took away the support they had once counted on.

"It's not just us," he muttered, almost to himself. "I see people—old friends from around town. They can't keep up either. People keep leaving. And here we are, trying to keep this place open, just barely hanging on."

She didn't know what to say, so she just nodded, her throat tight with the knowledge that they were sinking, and there was nothing she could do to save them.

Late that night, as she lay in her childhood bed, the walls closing in around her, she heard them. Her parents were in their room, the quiet murmurs of their voices drifting through the walls, growing louder, more desperate.

"It's getting worse, Frank," her mother whispered, her voice trembling. "Every day, the prices go up. People are getting angry. They're leaving. They're—Frank, I don't know how much longer we can keep this place going."

Her father's voice was strained, weary. "We'll find a way. We've always found a way."

"We can't keep raising prices," her mother replied, her voice cracking. "People can barely afford to come here as it is. Mrs. Rodriguez had to put her milk back today, Frank. She apologized, said she just couldn't pay that much. She's been coming here for twenty years. What are we supposed to do?"

There was a long silence. Amara could imagine her father's face, the pain in his eyes, the helplessness he tried so hard to hide.

"We promised her a better life," her mother continued, her voice breaking. "We promised Amara we'd give her a future. She's back here, and I—I feel like we've failed her."

Amara pressed her hand to her mouth, trying to hold back the sob that threatened to escape. She hadn't known. She hadn't realized how deeply her failure hurt them, how much they had pinned their hopes on her.

The next day, Amara tried to carry on as if she hadn't heard anything, helping her father stock shelves, greeting customers with a forced smile. But every word from the night before echoed in her mind. She saw the way her parents handled each transaction, apologizing to frustrated customers as they explained yet another price increase. She could see the sadness in her mother's eyes, the tension in her father's jaw as he struggled to hold it together.

As she bagged groceries for an elderly man, his hands trembling as he counted out coins for a few items, she felt a surge of anger at the world that had turned its back on people like her parents, people who had worked their whole lives only to be abandoned.

That night, her father sat at the kitchen table, his head in his hands, surrounded by a stack of bills. She could see the fear in his eyes as he stared at the numbers, trying to find a way to make it all work.

"They raised the interest rates again," he muttered, his voice barely above a whisper. "How do they expect us to keep up?"

Her mother sat across from him, her face drawn, her hands wringing a dish towel as she tried to hold back her own fears. "It wasn't supposed to be like this, Frank," she whispered, her voice thick. "This store… this store was supposed to be for her, for Amara. We wanted her to have something—something more."

Amara stood in the doorway, listening, her heart breaking with every word. She wanted to tell them it would be okay, that somehow, they'd find a way through this. But she knew the truth. They were drowning, and she was a part of it, another weight dragging them down.

The days turned into weeks, each one blending into the next. The shelves grew barer, the customers fewer. Amara's family's store, once a place people came for warmth and familiarity, was slipping into something hollow, a ghost of what it had once been. The familiar faces she'd known all her life drifted away, choosing the chain stores where prices were lower, where there were no apologies over the cost of milk.

One evening, as her father counted the day's earnings with trembling hands, she saw the despair in his eyes. He looked up at her, his voice barely a whisper. "I thought we'd be okay, Amara. I thought… I thought we'd find a way."

And in that moment, she felt the weight of everything they had worked for, everything they had sacrificed, pressing down on her like a weight she couldn't bear. She had dreamed of law school, of changing the world, but now she couldn't even change her own family's fate.

As the store emptied and the silence grew heavier, Amara felt her dreams fade, replaced by a quiet, endless despair. They had given her everything, and now there was nothing left to give.

And as the final light flickered out, she knew that the world she'd believed in, the promises they'd held onto, were gone, leaving only the broken pieces of a life that could never be mended.

ELEVEN

Harvey shuffled down the empty sidewalk, clutching a worn photograph in his hand, his fingers trembling as he brushed over the faded faces. He squinted, trying to make sense of the smiling people in the picture. The young man in uniform was him—that much he was almost sure of. He could still feel the weight of those years, the pride in serving, the long nights and sand-filled days. Next to him was a woman with soft curls, her hand resting on his shoulder, her face lit with a love that was… familiar. He could feel it in his chest, a tug, like something he'd known once, something that felt like home.

"Amy…" he whispered, the name slipping from his lips like a memory he couldn't hold onto. *Yes, that was it.* She was his wife. He tried to bring her face into focus, tried to feel her warmth, but she was slipping away from him, like sand falling through his fingers. And beside her—he looked harder, straining to remember—their daughter. A baby, bundled up in Amy's arms. *But what was her name?*

It was there, just at the edge of his mind, taunting him. He clenched his fist, the photo crumpling in his grip as he whispered, "I'm sorry… I'm trying to remember. I know I should…" The pain of it twisted in his chest, a knife buried deep, because he could feel her slipping further and further from him. His own daughter, and he couldn't remember her name.

He blinked, and suddenly the street around him didn't look right. Hadn't he been somewhere else just a moment ago? A place with nurses, with bright lights and careful voices telling him he was safe, that they would help him? The VA—yes, he'd been there. They'd told him he'd be looked after, given him words he could barely follow, but words he'd clung to like a lifeline. Now those halls felt like a distant dream, closed off and cold, the doors shut behind him. They'd told him there were "changes," that he had to "find a new provider." He didn't know what any of it meant. He just knew that they'd left him, sent him away with papers he couldn't read and numbers he couldn't dial.

"Where am I supposed to go?" he murmured, the words falling into the cold, empty air around him. He reached out, as if he might grasp some sense of direction, but the streetlights only cast long, empty shadows, and he felt himself swallowed up in them.

He took a few uncertain steps, each one heavier than the last, his legs stiff and aching. His mind drifted again, slipping into places he couldn't quite hold onto. He was back in the desert, the heat pressing down on him, sand swirling around as he looked out over the horizon, his men at his side. He could hear the shouts, the rumble of distant explosions, the weight of his rifle heavy in his hands. He'd promised them they'd be safe, that he'd lead them home. They had looked at him with trust, with loyalty, like he was their rock, their anchor. But now, here he was, alone, a man who could barely remember his own name half the time.

His heart raced, panic rising in his chest as he tried to pull himself back, tried to remember where he was. The desert faded, replaced by empty sidewalks and faces of strangers who looked right through him, their eyes filled with indifference. He reached out to one, a man walking briskly, looking solid, familiar, like he might understand.

"Please, I'm… I'm trying to find my way. Can you—"

The man barely glanced at him, muttering something under his breath before hurrying off. Harvey stared after him, a burning anger and helplessness churning in his stomach. Once, people had listened to him, they'd respected him, they'd trusted him to lead them. Now he was nothing more than an old man, a stranger on the street, someone people turned away from.

He slumped onto a bench, the cold metal biting into him as he tried to gather himself, his hands shaking as he stared down at the photo again. Amy's face stared back at him, her smile soft and familiar, but fading, like a ghost that only appeared in half-light. He could almost hear her laugh, feel the warmth of her hand on his cheek, the way she'd tell him he was home now, that he was safe. She'd promised to always be there, to see him through. But she wasn't here, and he couldn't remember where she'd gone.

And their daughter… oh, their daughter. Her face hovered in his mind, blurry and out of reach, like something he'd once known by heart but could no longer touch. He could hear her laughter, faint and distant, the sound of her running through the house, her voice calling out to him with a name he could no longer recall. His little girl. His heart ached with the emptiness of it, the shame of forgetting his own child, the one he'd sworn to protect.

"I'm sorry," he whispered, his voice breaking, as though he could speak across the void, reach out to her wherever she was. "I'm sorry, baby… I don't know why I can't remember. I just… I don't know…"

He held the photo to his chest, closing his eyes, trying to hold onto the pieces of his life, but they were slipping, falling away from him, leaving him in darkness.

A memory bubbled up, bright and sharp—a warm kitchen, the smell of pancakes and coffee, sunlight streaming in as Amy danced around him, laughing, her arms around his neck. She'd always known how to keep him steady, how to pull him back when the world tilted. And their daughter—he could almost see her, could almost hear her little voice, high and sweet, asking for syrup with her pancakes, tugging at his sleeve. She'd looked at him with those big eyes, like he was her hero, like he was someone worth looking up to.

But the memory twisted, the edges fraying, and he felt it slipping, like a light fading into shadow. He opened his eyes, and the warmth was gone, replaced by the harsh glow of streetlights and the chill of night. He looked around, blinking, disoriented. Where was he supposed to go? He thought he'd known, thought there'd been a place, a building with nurses and kind faces who promised him he'd be safe. But that place was gone, too, locked away, closed off, and he was left wandering in a world that no longer made sense.

The cold seeped deeper, into his bones, his hands numb as he clutched the photo, the last piece of a life he could barely remember. He wanted to call out, to beg someone to help him, to guide him, to show him where he was supposed to be. He tried to picture Amy, her soft smile, the way she'd held him close when he was lost, whispering that he'd always have a place with her. But even that memory was fading, dissolving into the fog that filled his mind.

A tear slipped down his cheek, and he didn't bother to wipe it away. He could feel himself slipping, piece by piece, as though he were being erased from the inside out. His daughter's name echoed faintly in his mind, but he couldn't hold onto it, couldn't keep her face, her voice, her laughter. She was slipping away, too, and the pain of it tore at him, a sorrow so deep he thought it might break him.

"Please…" he whispered into the empty night, his voice barely audible. "Please… don't let me forget her. Don't let me lose her…"

But there was no answer, no comfort, just the silence of the empty streets, the cold pressing in, indifferent to his pleas.

Hours later, as dawn began to break, Harvey sat on the bench, his hands limp, the photograph lying crumpled at his feet. He stared at it, the faces blurring, fading, until he couldn't tell who they were anymore. He felt hollow, emptied out, as though he'd lost the last pieces of himself, as though he were nothing more than a shadow drifting through a world that had left him behind.

In the faint light, he closed his eyes, his mind slipping one last time into the memory of her face, her smile, her voice saying his name. And then, slowly, even that was gone, leaving him with nothing but silence, and the cold, unyielding ache of being truly, utterly alone.

TWELVE

Mark's hands shook as he gripped Ben's across the kitchen table, his knuckles white, his gaze locked on the floor. Words had dried up between them, replaced by a silence so thick it felt like drowning. A sense of unreality hung over the room, an emptiness that had crept in the day the letter came and never left. They'd read it together, sitting right here, their hands trembling, unable to look at each other as they took in what it meant.

It was just a piece of paper. Just a notice from some office somewhere, stamped and signed by a judge who would never know them, never see Lily's face or understand what she meant to them. But in a few brief, clinical sentences, the paper had stripped them of everything that made their lives matter. Their marriage—the life they'd built—was erased, dissolved in the eyes of the law. And now they were marked, branded as an "unsafe" influence on their daughter, stripped of their rights, their humanity, and left with nothing but this dark, suffocating silence.

Ben's hand tightened in Mark's, his thumb brushing over Mark's fingers with a kind of desperation, a plea for grounding in a world that had slipped out from under them. When he finally spoke, his voice was a broken whisper, raw and hoarse.

"She doesn't know, Mark. She doesn't know that everything's changed." He swallowed, his face creased with pain. "She still believes in us. She thinks we're her dads and that… and that we'll keep her safe." His voice cracked on the last word, the weight of it bearing down on him until he had to look away.

Mark clenched his jaw, his mind flashing back to Lily's last bedtime, her tiny arms wrapping around his neck, her sleepy smile as she whispered, "Goodnight, Daddy." She'd been so small, so innocent, clutching her teddy bear like it could keep the monsters away. She had no idea that the real monsters were waiting outside, lurking in the laws that had turned their lives into a nightmare.

"She's our daughter, Ben. She's ours. We raised her. We love her. And they think they can just… take her? Like she's a piece of property they can repossess?" Mark's voice rose, thick with fury and helplessness. "It's wrong. God, it's so wrong."

Ben's lips quivered as he tried to hold back the tears that were threatening to spill over. He nodded, his voice barely a whisper. "I don't understand… how can they say we're unfit? We've done everything for her. Everything." His shoulders shook, a quiet sob escaping him. "She's our world, Mark. And they're going to rip her out of it, like none of it ever mattered."

The memory of the clinic visit twisted inside Ben like a knife. He'd taken Lily in when her fever spiked, terrified it could be something serious. But the nurse had looked at him with contempt, her lips a thin, disapproving line as she'd said, "We don't treat your kind here."

Ben had felt the floor tilt beneath him, a rush of shame and anger swallowing him whole as he'd gathered Lily in his arms, her hot little body limp against him, her eyes glazed with confusion. He'd driven for hours, stopping at clinic after clinic, only to be told each time that there was no room, no help, nothing for him, nothing for them.

The shame had festered, a dark, ugly thing he'd carried back home, and that night, as he'd sat beside Mark on Lily's bed, watching her breathe, feeling her fever break, he'd wanted to scream, to break something, to fight back against a world that was quietly, methodically, erasing them.

The knock on the door interrupted the silence, each bang heavy and unyielding, echoing through the house. Mark's jaw tightened as he stood, his face a mask of grim determination, his fists clenched at his sides.

"Mark… what if they don't… what if we can't…" Ben's voice broke, his gaze darting to the hallway where Lily's bedroom door stood slightly ajar.

"She's ours, Ben. I won't let them take her." Mark's voice was low, steely, each word filled with a barely restrained fury.

He moved to the door, his steps slow and deliberate, as if each one was carrying him toward an execution. He glanced back at Ben, who was sitting rigid at the table, his hands trembling, his face etched with fear. Just as Mark reached for the doorknob, a small voice cut through the silence.

"Daddy?" Lily's voice was groggy, her small figure appearing in the hallway, clutching her teddy bear.

Ben's heart shattered at the sight of her. "Go back to bed, sweetheart," he said, his voice shaking. "Daddy and I… we're just talking to some people."

But Lily didn't move. She stood there, eyes wide, looking between them, sensing something in the air, an unease she didn't understand. Mark opened the door to reveal two officers standing on the porch, their faces blank, expressionless.

"Mark Roberts?" one of them asked, his voice cold and formal.

"Yes," Mark replied, his voice thick with barely restrained anger.

"We're here to enforce a court order. Your household has been deemed an unsafe environment for the minor, Lily Roberts, and she is to be placed in a state-approved facility."

Ben's voice broke as he stepped forward, pleading. "Please… you don't understand. She's our daughter. We've raised her. She's safe here."

The officer's gaze didn't waver. "Sir, if you do not comply, we are authorized to use force."

And in that moment, something inside Mark snapped. He lunged forward, his hand grabbing the officer's collar, shoving him back with a surge of raw fury. "You're not taking her!" he roared, his voice hoarse, filled with a desperation that had nowhere else to go. "She's ours. She's our daughter!"

The officer staggered, reaching for his belt, but Mark didn't stop. His fists swung, connecting with the officer's jaw, his vision red with rage. Behind him, he could hear Ben's panicked voice calling out, pleading, but he couldn't stop.

"Sir! Stand down!" The second officer's hand went to his sidearm, his voice sharp, cold. "I said, stand down!"

But Mark didn't hear him. All he could see was Lily, her small face frozen in terror, her eyes wide as she clutched her bear, watching her fathers fight to protect her.

Then came the crack of the gunshot.

Mark's body jolted as the bullet struck his chest, a searing pain tearing through him. He staggered, his knees buckling, his hand instinctively going to the wound as he fell. The world blurred around him, his vision narrowing to the one thing that mattered: Lily, her small form trembling, her face twisted with horror.

"Daddy! They shot my daddy!" Lily's voice was a scream, raw and broken, piercing the air as she tried to run toward him, but the second officer grabbed her, holding her back as she fought, her cries echoing off the walls. "Daddy, help! Daddy, please!"

Ben surged forward, but the first officer restrained him, twisting his arms behind his back, forcing him to the ground as he struggled, his voice a guttural, broken sob.

"Mark! Mark, no! Let me go! Please, let me go to him!"

The officers held him firm, his face pressed against the floor, his cries muffled as he watched Mark lying on the ground, each ragged breath more labored, his eyes slipping in and out of focus.

"Lily…" Mark's voice was barely a whisper, his hand reaching out, fingers trembling as he tried to reach her. His vision was darkening, the edges blurring, but he forced himself to look at her, to hold on to the last piece of his world.

"Daddy, please! Don't let them take me!" Lily's small voice trembled with terror as the officer began pulling her toward the door, her little hands reaching out, desperately grasping for him, for Ben, for anything that would keep her here, keep her safe.

Ben's scream filled the room, raw and unrestrained, his face contorted with a pain so deep it was almost primal. "Please, don't take her! She's our daughter! Don't take her!"

But the officers were unmoved, their faces hard as they pulled Lily away, her cries fading as they led her out into the night. Mark's breaths were shallow, his eyes dimming, his hand falling to the floor as the darkness closed in.

The last thing he saw was Lily's face, tear-streaked and filled with terror, disappearing into the night.

And then, silence.

Ben lay on the floor, his body wracked with sobs as he watched the light die from his husbands eyes, the world around him empty, hollow, the weight of loss pressing down on him like a physical force. Everything they'd built, everything they'd fought for, had been taken from him, leaving him alone in a world that had erased his family, his love, his life.

All that was left was a hollow, aching void, a silence that would never be filled, and the memory of a love that had been torn from him, leaving him broken, clinging to nothing but the fragments of what once was.

THIRTEEN

Subject: *Possible Case of Illness in Town*
From: *clinic.manager@smalltowndoctors.org*
Date: August 5, 2025
To: *regional.health@fed.gov*

Hello,

I hope this message finds the correct person. We've recently
seen a few patients come into our clinic with symptoms that
don't quite fit into anything we're familiar with—fever, joint
pain, extreme fatigue, and, in a few cases, a red rash that
appears on the torso and spreads to the limbs. At this time,
the cases seem isolated to one neighborhood, but it's hard to
be certain without the ability to test or trace contacts more
widely.

With the recent federal changes affecting our budget, we're
doing our best but are limited in diagnostics and
preventative measures. If this falls under any advisory or
tracking protocols, could you let me know? I'd like to stay
proactive if this is a potential public health issue.

Thank you,
Dr. Jeanine Codswell
Harper Community Clinic

Subject: *Re: Unusual Symptoms Increasing—Follow-up Needed*
From: *clinic.manager@smalltowndoctors.org*
Date: August 15, 2025
To: *regional.health@fed.gov*

Hello again,

I'm following up on my previous email. In the past ten days, more patients have presented with similar symptoms, including fever, body aches, and the rash—although it now seems to be spreading beyond the torso, in some cases even forming blisters. Most of the patients are from different neighborhoods now, and it's beginning to feel less isolated. We've gone from two cases to nearly twenty.

I've tried to reach other clinics in our region by phone to see if they're experiencing anything similar, but calls don't seem to be going through reliably. I don't know if this is due to the recent changes in our area's cell tower policies, but it's making coordination difficult.

Without supplies or additional staff, it's becoming challenging to keep up. Please let us know if you have any guidance.

Best regards,
Dr. Jeanine Codswell
Harper Community Clinic

Subject: *Rising Case Numbers and Escalating Symptoms*
From: *clinic.manager@smalltowndoctors.org*
Date: August 26, 2025
To: *regional.health@fed.gov*

To Whom It May Concern,

We are now facing a concerning escalation. There are now over fifty patients in our town, all with similar symptoms: fever, a spreading rash that blisters, and some report trouble breathing. Some patients, including children, have developed severe symptoms that resemble pneumonia. Without access to proper testing facilities, we're unable to determine if this is viral or bacterial. All we know is that it's spreading fast.

I understand that certain health services in rural areas have been reorganized, but I'm reaching out to anyone who might offer assistance. With nearby clinics difficult to reach due to the inconsistent phone service, we are very isolated here. Internet service has also become intermittent, making communication challenging.

We need help urgently—medications, protective equipment, and if possible, guidance on isolating cases to prevent further spread. Please respond at your earliest convenience.

Sincerely,
Dr. Jeanine Codswell
Harper Community Clinic

Subject: *Outbreak Escalation—Critical Situation*
From: *clinic.manager@smalltowndoctors.org*
Date: September 3, 2025
To: *regional.health@fed.gov*

I'm reaching out once more with a serious update. The illness continues to spread, now affecting whole families. Children and the elderly seem particularly vulnerable. We've had parents bring in kids as young as four with high fevers and intense rashes that spread and blister. Two children are now experiencing severe respiratory distress, and I don't know how long we can keep them stable.

Some families are reluctant to bring their children in, as they've lost insurance coverage. It breaks my heart to see parents hesitate over medical care because they fear the cost. Our clinic is doing what it can, but we're limited on supplies, and the lack of outside support is making this exponentially harder.

I've attempted to contact local hospitals, but our calls are either dropped or simply don't connect. There are no direct lines to the support systems we once had, and it's as though Harper has been left to manage on its own.

Please respond with guidance or assistance. I can't overstate the urgency here.

Sincerely,
Dr. Jeanine Codswell
Harper Community Clinic

Subject: *Critical Condition: Fatalities Reported, Urgent Assistance Needed*
From: *clinic.manager@smalltowndoctors.org*
Date: September 10, 2025
To: *regional.health@fed.gov*

To Whom It May Concern,

The situation in Harper has worsened considerably. Over the past week, we've lost three patients—two elderly and one middle-aged man. All displayed severe respiratory symptoms, high fevers, and open sores from the rashes. Families are reeling, and we're stretched to breaking point. More patients come in each day with worsening symptoms, and I fear this illness has taken root in the town.

Without proper communication channels, we're unable to coordinate any regional response. I can't tell if our calls are failing due to local restrictions or the overwhelmed network, but this isolation is turning into a dangerous barrier to our efforts. We're out of basic antibiotics and wound care supplies, and I've begun rationing masks and gloves for staff.

This clinic cannot handle much more on its own. I beg for any resources or communication from your office. If you can read this, please understand: we're on the edge of a full breakdown.

Dr. Jeanine Codswell
Harper Community Clinic

Subject: *Crisis: Community Spread Uncontrolled, Town in Panic*
From: *clinic.manager@smalltowndoctors.org*
Date: September 17, 2025
To: *regional.health@fed.gov*

I'm writing once again, hoping this message gets through. The infection is now tearing through families, and we've run out of space to isolate cases effectively. We're seeing entire households coming down with fever, rashes, and breathing issues. Some rashes have become infected, and we have nothing left to treat secondary infections.

With our internet access as unreliable as it's been, I have no idea if these messages are even reaching you. Our cell coverage, too, has been spotty at best, leaving us unable to communicate with any nearby facilities.

People are frightened. They're questioning why there's no outside help coming, why they can't reach local officials or other medical facilities. They're looking to us for answers, and all we have are apologies and dwindling resources. I'm reaching out on behalf of every person in Harper, asking for a response, guidance, anything to help us make it through.

Thank you,
Dr. Jeanine Codswell
Harper Community Clinic

Subject: *Emergency: Total Collapse Imminent*
From: *clinic.manager@smalltowndoctors.org*
Date: September 28, 2025
To: *regional.health@fed.gov*

To anyone reading,

This will likely be my last attempt to reach out. We've lost six more people over the past two weeks, including two children. The symptoms are relentless—fevers, severe respiratory distress, blistering rashes that turn into open wounds. We're helpless to stop the spread.

Our supplies are gone, and I've begun turning away new patients, a decision I never imagined I would face. The town is panicking. People are searching for answers, wondering why they've been left to fend for themselves. Families mourn loved ones without understanding what went wrong. They're desperate, demanding answers I don't have.

I'm not sure if anyone will read this, but if you do, know that Harper needed help—and that we did everything we could with what we had. Please remember our community.

Dr. Jeanine Codswell
Harper Community Clinic

FOURTEEN

Rick sat in the hospital waiting room, staring at the tiled floor. The hum of the vending machines, the quiet rustle of newspapers, the muffled voices of other families—it all faded into a dull, numbing haze. The doctor's words still echoed in his head, each syllable like a stone dropped into a deep, dark well: "Without coverage, there's not much more we can do."

Shane was only nine years old, a bright, brave boy who'd always met life with a smile and a laugh, even after his diagnosis three years ago. Rick's chest tightened as he remembered his son's laughter, the light in his eyes, how fiercely he held onto hope. Diagnosed with a rare autoimmune disorder at six, Shane had endured more in a few years than most people would in a lifetime. His love for superheroes, his dreams of hitting a home run someday—they kept him going.

But lately, that spark had dimmed, and Rick could see the sickness taking more from him each day.

Medicaid had once covered Shane's medication and treatments, but in recent months, their world had turned upside down. Due to funding cuts and policy shifts, the program was gone, leaving Rick and Marie without the lifeline they'd clung to. Every option Rick had pursued had led nowhere: applications, emails, late-night phone calls to agencies and charities. They all ended the same way. "We regret to inform you…"

He'd felt the walls closing in, each rejection a nail sealing their fate. And as he sat in that sterile waiting room, exhaustion settled over him like a fog. He thought of Marie at home, sitting by Shane's bedside, her hand resting on his small, fragile shoulder as she murmured soft reassurances. They hadn't slept in days, and that morning, as Rick had left, Marie had clutched his hand, her eyes hollow with worry.

"We have to find a way, Rick," she'd whispered, her voice barely holding together. "He's slipping away. We can't just sit by and watch him… fade."

Her voice haunted him, those words cutting through his thoughts like a knife. Sitting there, his head bowed, the weight of it all pressing down on him, an idea began to take root—a quiet, terrifying thought that had lingered in his mind over countless sleepless nights. It was born out of pure desperation, the hopeless hours spent watching his son grow weaker, his wife grow more afraid. It grew, piece by piece, until it was the only thing left.

He had no choice.

The streets were quiet as Rick pulled his car up a block away from the small, downtown bank. The day was already fading, casting long shadows across the asphalt. His hands gripped the steering wheel, his knuckles white, his breath coming in short, shallow gasps. He could feel the weight of the pistol in his jacket pocket—an old revolver he hadn't touched in years. It was just for show, he told himself, a reassurance, something he'd never need to use. He wasn't here to hurt anyone. He was just a father trying to save his son.

He glanced down, adjusting his hood, trying to calm the frantic beat of his heart. Images of Shane flashed through his mind, lying pale and fragile in that dimly lit bedroom, his breaths growing weaker, his eyes distant and tired. The pain, the helplessness, the knowledge that he'd tried every other way to help his son—all of it surged through him as he stepped out of the car.

Inside the bank, the air was filled with the low hum of activity— quiet conversations, footsteps, the faint beeping of machines. Rick walked to the counter, every nerve on edge, his hands trembling as he slid a crumpled note across to the young woman standing behind the glass. She looked up at him, her face shifting from casual politeness to fear as she took in his hooded figure, the tension in his eyes.

"Please," he said, his voice barely above a whisper. "Put the money in the bag. I don't want to hurt anyone… I just need it."

Her hands began to shake as she read the note, her face pale. He watched as her fingers fumbled with the stacks of bills, her eyes darting toward the silent alarm. Rick's chest tightened, the guilt twisting like a knife, but he forced himself to hold steady. He was here for Shane, for the boy who had fought so hard, so bravely. There was no turning back.

"It's for my son," he said, his voice breaking, as if trying to explain, to justify. "He's sick… dying. This… this is my only option."

Her face softened, if only for a moment, and she looked down, slipping the last stack of bills into the bag with shaking hands. Just as she passed the bag across the counter, the front door swung open, and a commanding voice cut through the silence like a knife.

"Stop right there! Hands where I can see them!"

Rick's heart seized, his mind blanking as he turned, his stomach dropping as he saw the officer standing at the entrance, gun drawn, his face a mask of grim determination.

Rick's heart pounded, the officer's shout echoing in his ears. In a flash of panic, he grabbed the bag, but just as he turned to run, a gunshot cracked through the air. He froze, his body tense, and he heard the young teller scream as she fell to the floor, her body crumpling, blood spreading across the tiles.

The officer shouted again, but Rick bolted for the emergency exit. The bag slipped from his hands as he stumbled, cash spilling out, bills scattering across the floor, falling around him like leaves. His heart hammered, the horror of what had just happened crashing over him.

A second shot rang out, grazing his shoulder with a sharp, searing pain, but he forced himself forward, pushing through the door and stumbling into the alley. The pain throbbed, but he kept running, his mind consumed with fear and guilt. He'd lost everything—the money, the hope, the chance to save his son. And the young woman's face, her scream, her blood, haunted him, a shadow he couldn't escape.

It was past midnight when Rick finally returned home, his shoulder throbbing, his body weak, his hands shaking. He crept inside, hoping to make it to the bathroom unseen, to wash away the blood, the shame, the failure. But as he stepped into the dim hallway, Marie emerged from Shane's room, her face pale, her eyes widening as she took in his disheveled appearance, the blood on his shirt.

"Rick…" Her voice was barely a whisper, filled with a tremor of fear. She took a step forward, her hand reaching out, brushing against his bloodied shoulder. "What… what happened?"

Rick tried to turn away, the shame and guilt weighing down on him, but Marie's grip tightened, her face filled with horror. "Rick, what did you do?" Her voice broke, the fear raw in her eyes.

He couldn't meet her gaze. His throat tightened, the words caught, heavy, in his chest. "I… I tried, Marie," he managed, his voice rough, broken. "I tried everything. But… it wasn't enough."

Her face crumpled, her hand covering her mouth as she stumbled back, her shoulders shaking. She stared at him, as if seeing a stranger, and he felt his heart splinter, his soul laid bare.

Without another word, he turned and walked to the bathroom, shutting the door behind him. He leaned against the sink, staring at his reflection in the mirror. His bloodstained shirt, his hollow, haunted eyes—he barely recognized himself. He stripped off his clothes, his body numb as he stepped into the shower, the hot water pouring over him, washing away the blood but doing nothing to cleanse the shame.

He sank to his knees, his shoulders hunched, his face in his hands as the reality hit him, each wave of guilt and failure crashing over him. He had risked everything, sacrificed everything, and it still hadn't been enough. He'd failed Marie. He'd failed Shane. And now, the horror of what he'd done clung to him, a weight he couldn't bear.

The sobs broke free, raw and desperate, tearing from him in heaving gasps as he grieved for the life he couldn't save, the life he'd ruined. He stayed there, hunched under the water, letting it pour over him until it ran cold, until his body went numb.

When he finally emerged, dressed in fresh clothes, Marie was waiting for him in the hallway, her face etched with worry, her eyes searching his. She didn't ask, didn't press. She simply took his hand, her grip steady, grounding, and led him down the hall to Shane's room.

Shane lay in bed, his face pale, his breaths shallow, his small body swallowed up by the blankets. Rick knelt beside him, reaching out to take his son's hand, feeling the warmth that was slipping away, the light dimming.

Shane's eyes fluttered open, a faint smile touching his lips as he looked up at his father. "Hey, Dad…" he whispered, his voice soft, tired.

Rick's heart clenched, the tears burning in his eyes as he forced a smile. "Hey, buddy," he murmured, his voice thick. He looked at Shane's face, so small, so fragile, and felt his heart shatter.

"where were you…are you okay?" Shane's voice was barely audible, his eyes filled with quiet trust, the hope that only a child could hold.

Rick nodded, swallowing back the grief that clawed at his chest. "Yeah, buddy," he whispered, his voice breaking. "everything is fine. Just close your eyes… rest now."

Shane's eyelids drooped, his small hand curling around Rick's, his breaths slowing as he slipped into sleep. Rick sat beside him, feeling the weight of everything he'd lost, the unbearable hollow ache that filled the room. When the first light of dawn began to slip through the window, casting a pale glow over Shane's sleeping face, Rick felt the full weight of his failure settle over him like a shadow.

The room was quiet, the soft hum of Shane's breathing the only sound. Rick hadn't moved from his spot by Shane's bed, his hand still wrapped around his son's, holding onto the last bit of warmth, of hope, even as it faded.

The hollow ache grew, filling the space between heartbeats, a grief too vast to name. Slowly, he leaned forward, pressing a gentle kiss to Shane's forehead, lingering there for a moment, as if his touch could shield his son from all the hurt, the fear, the uncertainty that lay beyond these walls. But he knew it couldn't.

Rick finally let go, his fingers trembling as he released Shane's hand. He rose, feeling the weariness seep into his bones, the heaviness of a father's love that hadn't been enough.

Marie was waiting in the doorway, her face etched with sorrow and exhaustion. She held out her hand, and he took it, following her down the dim hallway, moving like a ghost in their own home. Together, they slipped into bed, their bodies lying side by side, the silence stretching between them like a chasm.

Marie turned on her side, curling into him, her hand resting over his chest, trying to offer comfort. But Rick stared at the ceiling, his eyes wide open, haunted by the images that refused to fade—the pale, terrified face of the teller, the blood spreading across the cold floor, the officer's shout, the scattering bills, like ashes falling from a fire already extinguished.

Beside him, Marie's breathing grew even, her body finally succumbing to sleep. But Rick stayed awake, trapped in the relentless loop of memory, of guilt. The weight of his choices pressed down on him, heavy and unforgiving, as he lay there, feeling the love he carried for his son—an ache that pulsed with every beat of his heart, even in the dark, even in the silence.

FIFTEEN

Judge William Harlan leaned back in his leather chair, surveying the cityscape from his chambers on the thirtieth floor. The skyline stretched out before him, golden with the afternoon sun, each high-rise and building catching the light. To him, it felt like a symbol of prosperity, of things aligning just as they should in the world. This was the America he'd always believed in—a place built on order, law, and values. And in the wake of Project 2025, he felt more aligned with his country than ever before.

He brushed a hand over his desk, stopping at the silver frame that held Emily's photograph—a candid shot from their honeymoon in Italy, her smile wide and eyes bright against a sunlit landscape. He never grew tired of looking at it, of remembering that moment. They'd been young, freshly married, and full of plans. That had been six years ago. Now, with Emily almost seven months pregnant, they were preparing for their greatest adventure yet: parenthood.

The thought of their son brought a warmth to his chest, a sense of fulfillment that made everything else seem small. It was as though each piece of his life was falling into place. He imagined the years ahead— teaching his son how to throw a baseball, seeing him off to school, eventually watching him grow into a man. This child would be his legacy, the promise of everything he'd worked for, everything he'd stood by. And in a world that felt more just, more ordered, he was certain that their son would grow up with the same values that had shaped his own life.

He checked his watch, realizing it was close to five. Maybe he'd go home early, surprise Emily, and take her out to dinner. She'd been a bit tired lately, her pregnancy weighing on her, but even so, she radiated a joy and calm that filled their home with light. He loved her for that—her steadiness, her kindness, the way she seemed to make everything feel easy, natural. And now, with a child on the way, it felt like they were at the pinnacle of something beautiful.

A knock at the door broke his thoughts, and he glanced up, somewhat annoyed by the intrusion. "Come in," he called, adjusting his tie, preparing to leave.

His clerk entered, his face pale, eyes wide with something like fear. "Judge Harlan…" He hesitated, his voice tight. "There's been… an emergency. Your wife, Emily. She's been taken to the hospital."

William felt the room spin, his heart lurching in his chest. "The hospital?" His voice came out strangled, his body already moving, grabbing his coat from the stand.

"Yes, sir," the clerk stammered, clearly shaken. "She… collapsed, they said. There were… complications."

"Complications?" The word felt foreign, out of place, an ill-fitting piece in the life he had so carefully built. He looked at the clerk, a dozen questions burning in his mind, but he couldn't speak. All he could think of was Emily, her gentle laugh, her hand resting on her rounded belly, her smile when she talked about their future. And now, she was in a hospital bed, somewhere between life and death.

Without another word, he bolted out of his chambers, the door swinging shut behind him. His footsteps echoed through the empty corridors as he rushed toward the elevator, barely hearing the concerned voices of his colleagues as he passed. He jabbed at the elevator button, his breath coming in short, panicked gasps. The polished metal doors opened, and he stepped inside, clutching his coat to his chest, trying to steady himself.

As the elevator descended, he felt a hundred thoughts swirl in his mind—fragments of memories, flashes of moments with Emily, moments they had shared, moments he feared he might lose. Her hands tracing patterns on his back in the dark, her quiet voice as they whispered about their son's future, her laugh as she watched him fumble with assembling the crib just a week ago.

The elevator doors opened, and he bolted toward the parking lot, fumbling for his keys, his mind in a haze. The drive to the hospital felt like a fever dream, the world blurring past in a streak of headlights and concrete. He barely registered the stoplights, the honking cars, his focus a singular, desperate need to reach her. His hands gripped the wheel, his knuckles white, his breath coming in short, shallow bursts.

Arriving at the hospital, he threw open his car door and rushed through the sterile halls, feeling as if he were caught in some surreal nightmare. The fluorescent lights cast everything in a sickly glow, and the antiseptic smell filled his nose, making him feel faint, off-balance.

A nurse met him outside the room, her face lined with worry, her voice soft. "Judge Harlan?"

He nodded, words caught in his throat. He could only stare at her, his mind blank, his body tense with dread.

She guided him into a small, private waiting room, gesturing for him to sit. "Your wife… Emily," she began, her tone gentle but firm. "There's been a severe complication. Her placenta detached prematurely."

Her words echoed in his mind, his heart pounding in his ears. He struggled to understand, to piece together what it all meant. "What… what does that mean?"

She hesitated, her eyes softening with sympathy. "It means that the baby has lost his blood and oxygen supply. I'm so sorry, but… there was nothing we could do. Your son… he didn't survive."

The words hit him like a punch to the chest, the air leaving his lungs. He closed his eyes, feeling the pain roll over him in waves, sharp and relentless. The image of his son, the life he'd imagined, all of it shattered in an instant.

He fought to breathe, forcing his mind to focus on Emily. She was still here. She was still alive. He gripped the armrest of the chair, his voice rough and desperate. "And… and my wife? Emily?"

The nurse's face fell, her eyes clouded with something like regret. She lowered her voice, leaning closer. "Judge Harlan, she's septic. The pregnancy caused an infection, and without immediate intervention, the risk to her life is…" She trailed off, letting the words hang in the air.

"But… then do it. Save her." His voice was barely a whisper, his heart racing as he looked at the nurse, waiting for her to explain the procedure, to give him some hope, some promise that Emily would survive.

Her eyes fell, and she glanced around before speaking again, her voice barely more than a whisper. "Sir, we would need to perform a removal of the fetal tissue. But under the recent laws… it's considered an abortion."

The word sounded hollow, cold, a blade driven between his ribs. "And?" he asked, his voice trembling. "She needs it. She'll die without it. You're telling me you can't perform the procedure?"

The nurse shifted, her expression pained. "I'm so sorry, sir. We can't. Not without a signed waiver proving non-viability from a state official."

The absurdity, the cruelty of it, hit him all at once. He was a judge, a man who had spent his life enforcing these very laws, yet here he was, trapped by them, helpless, unable to save the woman he loved.

The nurse left, her words trailing behind like shadows, filling the air with a terrible silence. William sat alone, numb, his mind struggling to process what he'd heard. Emily was septic. She was dying, and there was a procedure—simple, straightforward—that could save her. But because of the very laws he'd once championed, they couldn't touch her. Not legally.

He thought of every case he'd ever ruled on, every speech he'd given, each one dripping with certainty, with faith in a system he believed was just. But now, that same system held his wife in a death grip, bound by red tape and regulations he could barely understand. Each memory of his past convictions stung, mocking him, turning his own values into shackles.

He stood up, pacing the cold hospital hallway, his hands raking through his hair. His phone buzzed in his pocket, and for a moment, he thought it might be news—someone, somewhere, granting an exception. But it was just a text from a colleague, a casual update on the afternoon's docket. He wanted to throw the phone across the hall, to scream, to lash out at something, anything that could bear the weight of his grief.

Instead, he pocketed the phone, forcing his breaths to steady as he approached Emily's room. He paused outside the door, resting his hand on the cool, polished metal, gathering himself before stepping inside. When he finally opened the door, he felt the surge of sterile air hit him, carrying with it a bitter, antiseptic scent that made his throat tighten.

Emily lay on the bed, her skin pale, her face gaunt and shadowed. She looked up as he entered, her lips parting in a weak smile, her eyes tired yet filled with that same warmth, that same love he'd known for years. He swallowed back his emotions, forcing a smile for her, praying she couldn't see the fear in his eyes.

"Hey, sweetheart," he murmured, crossing the room to take her hand. Her fingers were cold, limp, but she squeezed his hand, her grip faint but steady.

"Will," she whispered, her voice so soft he had to lean close to hear. "Is everything… okay?"

He swallowed, nodding, his thumb brushing over her knuckles. "Yes, Em. Everything's fine." The words felt bitter, hollow, but he forced himself to say them. She didn't need to know. Not yet.

A faint shadow of worry crossed her face. "I… I heard them talking, Will. I know… I know they said there's a problem." She looked at him, her eyes pleading, searching. "Please… tell me what's going on."

He couldn't hold her gaze. His voice trembled as he forced the truth out, a soft whisper that hung in the air like a curse. "They… they can't do anything, Em. Because of the… the laws." His jaw tightened, his hands clenching around hers. "But I'm going to fix this. I promise you that."

She closed her eyes, a tear slipping down her cheek, her lips pressing into a faint smile. "I trust you," she murmured, her voice so soft it nearly broke him. She squeezed his hand again, her strength waning, her breaths shallow. "I trust you."

Over the next two days, he became a man possessed. He called every contact, every favor, every friend who had a foot in the door with the legislature. Each call, each desperate plea, met with the same empty, resigned response. "The law is the law, Judge Harlan. You of all people should know that." He'd heard it a dozen times, each one a blow, each one a reminder of his powerlessness.

At one point, he nearly stormed into the governor's office, demanding they make an exception, screaming for justice. But the security guards had stopped him in the lobby, ushering him out like a stranger, their eyes showing none of the respect he'd once taken for granted. It was surreal, like a nightmare where he was trapped in a foreign world that bore no resemblance to his own.

He returned to the hospital each night, sitting by Emily's bed, watching as her strength slipped away, her skin growing more pallid, her breaths shallow. She looked at him, her eyes filled with love, with unspoken words that cut him deeper than any wound. She smiled for him, her hand reaching out to brush his cheek, whispering, "It'll be okay. We… we had a good life, Will."

"Don't say that," he choked, gripping her hand, his voice barely holding together. "Don't you dare say that. I'm going to save you. I'm going to find a way."

But the resolve in his voice was hollow, empty. He was running out of options, out of time. And the brutal irony of it tore at him—the man who had once upheld the law with unshakeable certainty was now crushed beneath it, unable to save the woman he loved.

On the third night, he sat alone in his car, the hospital looming in the rearview mirror. The reality was closing in on him, a suffocating weight that pressed down on his chest, making it hard to breathe. And that's when he remembered a name—a whispered rumor he'd heard, a "doctor" who worked under the radar, taking cases that no one else would touch.

He had dismissed it as hearsay, something beneath him, irrelevant in his perfect world. But now, with Emily's life slipping through his fingers, it felt like his last hope, the one chance he couldn't afford to ignore. William sat in his car outside the unmarked building, his heart pounding, his hands shaking as he looked up at the dimly lit window on the second floor. This was it—his last hope. He'd made the call, he'd found a doctor willing to help, someone who would look the other way, who didn't care about laws or limitations, someone who could save her.

The entrance was shadowed, tucked behind a row of dumpsters. He swallowed his pride, his guilt, everything that had once made him Judge Harlan, and forced himself to move. He had no other choice.

Inside, the stairwell smelled of mildew and dust, each step creaking as he climbed. He reached the second floor and knocked, his knuckles white with tension. The door opened a crack, and an older man's eyes glinted in the shadows, looking him over with cold calculation.

"You the one who called?" the man asked, his voice low, unfeeling.

"Yes." William's voice was barely more than a whisper. He forced himself to keep his gaze steady, to show no fear, even as the shame clawed at him.

The man nodded, pushing the door open. "This isn't a charity, Judge. You've got my price?"

"Yes." William pulled a thick envelope from his jacket, handing it over. "Just… please. She's all I have."

The doctor counted the money, each bill slipping through his fingers like sand, like time running out. Finally, he looked up and gave a curt nod. "I'll see her tomorrow. But this stays between us. Understand?"

William nodded, his heart pounding with a flicker of hope. This was it. He had a plan, a way to save Emily. And for the first time in days, he allowed himself to believe, to imagine bringing her home, her laughter filling the halls again, her hand slipping into his, their life resuming as if this nightmare had never happened.

But as he turned to leave, the door behind him burst open. Bright lights filled the room, blinding him, and a dozen officers swarmed in, guns drawn, their faces set with grim determination.

"William Harlan, you're under arrest."

The words hit him like a sledgehammer. He stumbled back, his mind reeling, his heart lurching in his chest as they pulled his hands behind his back, cold steel snapping around his wrists. The doctor had vanished, his expression unreadable, his hands pocketing the money as he slipped into the shadows.

"No, no—wait!" William struggled against their hold, his voice rising in desperation. "You don't understand. My wife—she's dying! I just… I needed help!"

The officers ignored his pleas, dragging him through the building, out into the cold night air. The irony was a bitter poison in his mouth. He had spent years sentencing men like himself, men who had broken the law out of desperation, and now, here he was, trapped in the same cell of hypocrisy and helplessness.

As they placed him in the back of the police car, he felt his world crumbling, piece by piece, until there was nothing left but a hollow ache, a gnawing horror that filled every corner of his being. He sat in the cold metal seat, his head bowed, his mind consumed with images of Emily lying in that hospital bed, her life slipping away, waiting for him to save her.

Hours later, he sat alone in a dim, concrete cell, the silence stretching around him like a noose. The guards had ignored his pleas, his demands to make a call, to contact someone, anyone who could get him back to Emily. He had nothing—no phone, no one to turn to, no escape from the cage he had built for himself.

The other prisoners eyed him with curiosity, some with quiet satisfaction. He recognized a few of them—men he'd sentenced himself, men he'd condemned with the same laws that had now condemned him. One of them sneered, leaning close to the bars. "Well, well… look who's slumming it with the rest of us."

William ignored him, his mind a numb haze, his body slumped on the cold metal bench. He closed his eyes, the image of Emily haunting him, her face pale and drawn, her eyes filled with that fragile hope she'd placed in him. She had trusted him, believed in him. And he had failed her.

Hours passed, though it felt like an eternity, each second dragging on, hollow and endless. Finally, footsteps echoed down the corridor, heavy and deliberate, and a guard appeared at the cell door. William looked up, a flicker of hope sparking in his chest.

"Judge Harlan," the guard said, his voice a cold monotone. "Your wife… she didn't make it. We… found her in her hospital room."

The words struck like a knife, twisting deep, cutting through bone and flesh, leaving him breathless. He felt the world tilt, felt his heart shatter, the reality settling in, raw and brutal. Emily was gone. His beautiful, vibrant Emily, the woman who had filled his life with light, was dead. And he'd spent her final moments here, in this cell, surrounded by the same cold concrete he'd once sentenced others to.

A sob tore from his throat, raw and broken, the sound reverberating off the walls, filling the empty cell with the weight of his grief. The other prisoners looked away, their mocking smiles fading as they watched him, as they saw a man broken beyond recognition.

The guard's voice was faint, indifferent. "You have ten minutes for visitation. She's… in the morgue. If you want to see her."

He rose on shaky legs, following the guard down the long, sterile corridors, his steps unsteady, his heart a hollow ache that grew with each passing second. When they finally reached the morgue, he saw her—pale, still, her once-lively eyes closed forever.

He staggered to her side, reaching out with trembling hands, his fingers brushing over her cold skin, his mind reeling with grief, regret, the cruel irony that had led him here. He had once believed in justice, in law, in the power of his position. But now, he knew the truth—that all of it had been empty, that his faith had been nothing more than a mask for the system's cruelty.

He leaned over her, pressing a kiss to her forehead, his tears falling onto her still face, his heart breaking with every silent apology, every unspoken word. "I'm so sorry," he whispered, his voice choked with sorrow. "I'm so, so sorry."

As he pulled away, he felt the emptiness settle in, a deep, unrelenting void that he knew would haunt him for the rest of his life

SIXTEEN

Thomas Red Elk stood on the ridge, his eyes tracing the path of the river winding through the valley below. The land stretched wide beneath the setting sun, bathed in gold and shadow, but to him, it looked bruised, sickly. The water that had once flowed clear, bringing life to the people and land, was now tainted, a greenish-gray that rippled with toxic sheen. This river had sustained his ancestors, connected him to his heritage, his childhood, his roots. Now, it was dying, and with it, the last piece of what had once been theirs.

Beside him, his niece, Lila, stood silently, her eyes fixed on the murky river, her shoulders hunched, as if she were carrying the weight of a hundred generations. She didn't need to speak; he could feel the same grief and rage simmering within her, an ache they both shared—a betrayal deeper than words.

"It isn't just the river, Uncle," she said, her voice tight, trembling. "People are sick. Kids… they're coughing, breaking out in rashes. Mr. Grey Wolf's in the hospital. They think it's from the water." Her hands balled into fists, her eyes burning. "And we… we let them do this. We trusted them."

Thomas's jaw clenched, the shame gnawing at him. He had sat in those meetings, listened to the officials dressed in their crisp suits, their words smooth, practiced. They'd told them this was progress, that easing restrictions would allow for growth, for jobs, for a better future. They'd spoken of prosperity, of freedom, of putting power back into their hands. And for once, he had dared to believe it.

He had let himself hope, for the first time in years, that maybe this would be a new beginning. That his people, who had survived so much, who had fought for so long, could finally find a way forward. But it had all been a lie.

He swallowed, his throat tight, his voice barely more than a whisper. "They didn't care about us, Lila. They never did. All they cared about was the land, the resources, the profit. And we—" He shook his head, feeling the weight of his own foolishness pressing down on him. "We were just the price of doing business."

Lila's face twisted with anger, her voice rising as she looked out over the valley. "They poisoned our river, Uncle. The water is killing us. And all they care about is lining their pockets." She looked at him, her eyes filled with a bitter, aching sadness. "How could we let them do this? How could we trust them?"

The question cut deep, an accusation and a confession all at once. He had trusted them because he had wanted to believe that his people could finally have a say, that they could be part of the promise they'd been sold. But now, standing here, looking at the sickly water, he felt only shame. Shame that he had believed, shame that he had let himself be fooled, shame that he had cast his lot in with the same people who had taken everything from them before.

"We were foolish, Lila," he said softly, his voice hollow. "They said it was about self-reliance, about putting us in control. But the only thing they wanted was to take. And we handed it to them, believing they'd leave us with something worth keeping."

Her hands trembled, her eyes brimming with a mix of rage and grief. "It's happening again, isn't it?" Her voice cracked, barely holding back tears. "First, they took everything. And when there was nothing left, they gave us this land, as if they were doing us a favor. And now… now even this is being poisoned."

Thomas could barely meet her gaze. He looked down at the river, feeling the weight of history pressing down on him. His father had fished these waters, his grandfather had bathed in its cool depths. The river had been sacred, a bond with the past, a promise for the future. But now, all he could see was the slow, creeping death winding its way through the valley.

"People are scared," Lila continued, her voice thick with pain. "The kids… the kids ask if it's safe to drink the water, and I don't have an answer for them." She swallowed, her voice barely a whisper. "I feel like I'm lying to them, every time I tell them it'll be okay."

Thomas's chest ached, a deep, hollow ache that radiated through his bones. They had been given this land, not as a gift, but as an afterthought, a place that no one else wanted, a piece of the world that had been deemed worthless. And now, even that was being stripped from them, poisoned by policies that had rolled back protections, that had opened the door for factories to dump their waste, unchecked, into the water that sustained them.

He felt the burn of resentment twist in his gut, the bitter taste of regret mingling with the shame. "They said it was about 'freedom,'" he said bitterly, the word catching in his throat. "But what kind of freedom is this? The freedom to watch our children get sick? To see our elders suffer?"

He looked out over the valley, feeling the weight of his ancestors' disappointment, the silent accusation in the land itself. They had allowed this to happen, had trusted people who saw them as little more than obstacles, who valued profit over lives. And now, the river that had once been their salvation was their curse.

Lila's voice trembled, thick with unshed tears. "What are we supposed to do, Uncle? We tried calling for help—for someone to clean the water, to bring in clean supplies. But FEMA, the state, everyone just keeps saying the same thing: 'You're on your own.'" She looked away, her shoulders slumped, defeated. "What's left for us if even the land is turning against us?"

Thomas felt a wave of helplessness wash over him, the full, brutal reality of their situation settling in. There was no aid, no relief, no safety net. The programs that might have once provided help had been gutted, dismantled in the name of smaller government, of "freedom" and "independence." But it was a freedom that left them abandoned, left them to suffer alone.

"They gave us land they didn't want," he said softly, his voice filled with a quiet, aching bitterness. "And now, they're taking that too."

He closed his eyes, feeling the deep ache of betrayal, of heartbreak. This was all they had. This land, this river—it was supposed to be their sanctuary, their last piece of what had once been a life that stretched across these plains. And now, even that was slipping through their fingers, poisoned by the very people they had once trusted to bring prosperity.

They had been so hopeful, so eager to believe in the promises. But now, looking at the river, feeling the sting of the toxic air, he could only feel shame, a heavy, unrelenting shame that settled in his bones and refused to let go. Thomas and Lila stood in silence for a long moment, the poisoned river below a stark reminder of everything they'd lost, everything they had believed in, now turned against them. The air was thick, heavy with the metallic scent of pollution, a smell that had seeped into their homes, their lives, the very soil beneath their feet. Thomas could almost feel the land itself rejecting them, as if it knew they had failed to protect it.

Lila broke the silence, her voice low and strained. "I heard Mrs. White Feather is sick. She can barely walk anymore. The doctors say it's something in her blood—some kind of poison." She swallowed, looking down, her eyes filling with tears. "She was fine before. And now, it's like the land itself is… turning on her."

Thomas nodded, the familiar knot of anger and grief tightening in his chest. Mrs. White Feather had been a pillar of their community, a woman who had held their history, their traditions, as close to her heart as her own family. Now, she was bedridden, her body slowly giving out, poisoned by the water she had once called sacred. And she wasn't the only one.

Children were coughing through the night, their skin breaking out in rashes. Elders were falling ill, their bodies weakened by toxins no one could identify, no one could treat. The people were suffering, and all because they had been sold a lie, a promise of "freedom" that had only brought them closer to ruin.

"They won't help us, will they?" Lila's voice was barely more than a whisper. She looked at him, her face lined with despair, her eyes searching his for answers. "The ones we voted for, the ones who told us they'd make things better… they don't care, do they?"

Thomas felt the sting of her words, the truth cutting deeper than he cared to admit. He had voted for them too, had trusted that this time, the promises would mean something. But now, standing here, watching the river turn a sickly shade of green, he knew better. They were alone, abandoned by the very people who had claimed to be on their side.

"No," he said quietly, his voice filled with a quiet, resigned anger. "They don't care. They never did. All they wanted was profit, control. And we…" He took a shuddering breath, feeling the weight of his own complicity settle over him. "We gave it to them."

Lila's face crumpled, her fists clenching at her sides. "It feels like we betrayed ourselves. Like we… we chose this. And now our people are paying the price."

He looked down at her, his heart breaking as he saw the pain, the betrayal etched into her young face. She was too young to feel this kind of disillusionment, too young to carry the burden of broken promises and poisoned land. But there was nothing he could say, no words to ease her pain. She was right. They had chosen this. And now, they were living with the consequences.

He placed a hand on her shoulder, his grip firm, grounding them both. "We believed in something that wasn't real, Lila. We thought we could finally be part of a future that included us. But they were only using us. We were just a means to an end."

They stood together, uncle and niece, looking out over the valley that had once been their home, their sanctuary. The factories loomed on the horizon, their smokestacks pumping waste into the air, the runoff seeping into the river, poisoning everything in its path. The land that had once been a source of life, a place of healing and connection, was now a wasteland, a scar on the earth that they could never heal.

Lila shook her head, her voice filled with quiet despair. "They took everything from us, Uncle. And now, even what we had left… it's dying."

Thomas felt the sting of tears, the ache of loss that went beyond words. He thought of his father, his grandfather, the generations that had come before him, men who had watched their world change, who had seen their land taken piece by piece, promise by promise, until there was nothing left but this—this small, poisoned corner of the world, gifted to them like a consolation prize, a place to exist but never to thrive.

He closed his eyes, his hand still resting on Lila's shoulder, his heart heavy with a grief that felt as old as the land itself. "We have to remember, Lila. We have to hold on to what we have, even if it's just a memory."

She looked at him, her eyes brimming with tears, her voice barely more than a whisper. "But what do we have left to remember? The land is dying, the water is poisoned. Our people… they're getting sick. And there's no one to help us."

Thomas nodded, his own voice choked with sorrow. "I know. But we can't let them take everything from us. We have to keep our history, our stories, alive. We have to make sure our children know where we came from, what we fought for." He looked out over the valley, his gaze hardening. "Even if this land is taken from us, we can't let them take our spirit, our memory."

They stood in silence as the sun slipped below the horizon, casting the valley in shadow. The faint glimmer of the river reflected the last light of day, a sickly glow that spoke of death more than life. In that fading light, Thomas felt the full weight of their loss, a grief so deep it threatened to consume him.

But he held on, his hand on Lila's shoulder, a reminder of the bond they shared, of the legacy they carried. He couldn't undo what had been done, couldn't bring back the land they had lost, the promises that had been broken. But he could hold on to the memory, to the strength of his ancestors, to the spirit that had survived generations of betrayal.

SEVENTEEN

Peter Jones tightened his grip on the hose, his knuckles white beneath his gloves, as he watched the flames closing in. The sky above was thick with smoke, tinted an ominous, sickly shade of orange that cast an eerie glow over Wildwood Valley below. This fire was unlike anything he'd ever seen before. It moved with a ferocity, a hunger that seemed almost alive, leaping from tree to tree, devouring everything in its path. Every gust of wind sent embers swirling into the air, igniting the brittle, dry underbrush that stretched for miles.

They had all seen this coming—the drought, the relentless heat, the trees left standing dead after the logging companies stripped the hillsides bare. The townsfolk had begged for preventative measures, for firebreaks and updated equipment. But the funding had dried up, siphoned away in the name of "cutting red tape." And now, standing here, with the fire roaring toward them, Peter felt the weight of those decisions bearing down on him.

He turned to his crew, their faces streaked with soot and exhaustion. They were farmers and ranch hands who had volunteered to stand by him, men and women with no formal training but a fierce loyalty to their community. "Hold the line!" he shouted, his voice barely audible over the roar of the flames. "We don't let it through!"

The words felt hollow, a command he wasn't sure they could follow. The fire was relentless, driven by dry winds that swept through the valley, fueling the blaze as it raced toward Wildwood Valley. In the distance, he could just make out his own neighborhood, the small white house with the swing that Winter loved to sit on, kicking her legs as if she could touch the sky. He had promised Audrey he'd keep them safe, had reassured her with a confidence he no longer felt. "They'll send help if it gets bad," he'd told her, but now, watching the flames devour everything in their path, he knew he had lied.

His radio crackled to life, and for a moment, he felt a flicker of hope. Maybe backup was finally coming. But it was only static, a faint, garbled transmission that faded as quickly as it had come. There was no cavalry. The federal emergency funds had been gutted, and their small-town fire department was left to fend for itself.

He could see the worry in Eric's eyes as he took a step closer. "Peter... we're running on fumes. We can't hold this line."

Peter nodded, feeling the hopelessness claw at him. He could feel the heat pressing in, the flames so close he could hear them crackle, see the flicker of light reflecting in his crew's eyes. He looked back one last time, his gaze fixed on the distant outline of his own home, where Audrey and the kids were waiting, trusting that he would keep his promise to protect them.

"We hold it," he said, the words falling flat even as he spoke them. "We don't give up."

They positioned themselves, a thin line between the fire and the town, their bodies taut with fear and exhaustion. He thought of Audrey, of Peter Jr., of Winter, safe at home, or so he had told himself. But with every crackle, every rush of flames, he felt the creeping dread, the quiet voice in his mind whispering of danger, of loss, of the promises he could no longer keep.

One of his men stumbled back, tripping over a fallen branch as the fire leaped closer. Peter grabbed his arm, steadying him as he shouted, "Fall back to the trucks! Regroup, keep moving!"

But even as they retreated, even as they tried to keep their line, he knew it was too late. The fire was winning, its flames licking up the sides of houses, turning everything to ash. And somewhere in that inferno, his own home lay waiting.

They scrambled into the trucks, engines revving as they barreled down the road, the fire looming large in the rearview mirror. Peter's heart pounded, his mind racing as he thought of Audrey, of the kids, of the promises he had made. His hands shook as he gripped the wheel, his eyes fixed on the orange glow spreading across the town.

As they neared his street, Peter's heart sank. The fire had already reached his neighborhood, homes swallowed up in flames, structures collapsing under the heat. And then he saw it—his house, smoke billowing from the roof, flames creeping up the walls, turning the porch Audrey had painted herself to char.

He didn't think, didn't hesitate. He leapt from the truck, his feet pounding against the pavement as he sprinted toward the burning house. His mind was blank, his only thought to reach his family, to see them, to hold them, to make sure they were safe.

"Audrey!" he screamed, his voice raw, desperate. "Audrey! Winter! Peter!"

He stumbled through the front door, choking on the smoke as he forced his way inside. The heat was unbearable, flames dancing around him, consuming everything he had built, everything he had promised to protect. His mind raced, memories flashing before him—Winter's laugh, Peter Jr.'s tiny hand in his, Audrey's smile as she whispered that everything would be alright.

"Daddy!" a voice called out, faint, panicked. His heart clenched.

"Winter!" He turned toward the sound, forcing himself through the living room, where furniture had already begun to burn, flames curling around the walls. "Winter! I'm here!"

He found her huddled in the hallway, her face streaked with tears. She clung to him, her small arms wrapping around his neck as he lifted her, his heart pounding with relief.

"Where's Mommy? Where's Peter?" he asked, his voice barely audible over the roar of the flames.

"Mommy's… Mommy's trying to help Peter," she whispered, her voice trembling.

He pushed forward, his body aching, his lungs burning as he searched for them. And then he saw Audrey, cradling their son, her face streaked with soot as she tried to shield him from the heat.

"Peter!" Her eyes met his, filled with a raw, unspoken plea.

Without thinking, he reached out, pulling them into his arms, clutching them close as he forced his way toward the door, his heart racing with a desperate, frenzied determination. They moved together, step by step, inching toward the front door, toward safety.

But as they reached the entryway, the ceiling gave way, crashing down in a torrent of flames. Peter threw himself over his family, shielding them as best he could, his body wracked with pain, his vision fading as he fought to stay conscious.

"Peter…" Audrey's voice was a faint whisper, filled with a love that tore at his soul. "Get them… get them out…"

With a final burst of strength, Peter lifted his children, pushing them toward the door, his heart breaking as he watched Audrey slip from his grasp, her eyes meeting his one last time. The world around him blurred, his mind a haze of pain, loss, and a love so fierce it threatened to consume him.

Outside, his crew pulled the children from his arms, their voices muffled, distant, as he collapsed onto the pavement, his body spent, his soul shattered. He felt Eric's hand on his shoulder, heard the distant wail of sirens, but none of it mattered. All he could see was Audrey's face, her eyes filled with a love he would carry with him, a love that would haunt him long after the flames had faded.

As the paramedics lifted him, as the fire continued to rage, Peter felt a hollow emptiness settle in his chest, a grief so deep it threatened to drown him. He had believed in the promises, had trusted that they would be safe, that he could protect them. But as he watched the smoldering remains of his home, as he heard the cries of his children, he knew he had been wrong.

He had put his faith in a system that had abandoned him, that had stripped away the protections that might have saved them. And now, as the last light of his world faded to ash, he was left with nothing but the hollow echo of promises broken, a life destroyed.

EIGHTEEN

The crowd outside the Capitol was a sea of faces, each bearing a story, each marked by anger, desperation, and the scars of recent losses. Bethany stood on the front line, her hands gripping the edges of her sign, her knuckles white against the words she'd painted in furious strokes the night before: *Liberty Lost*. All around her, others raised signs and chanted, voices merging into a single, thunderous cry that echoed through the square. From where she stood, the Capitol building loomed, an impassive structure, silent and indifferent, but now faced with a force it hadn't anticipated.

To her right, she saw college students with tired faces, some of whom had traveled from across the country, hoping to raise their voices against the policies that had crushed their dreams of higher education. Some of them held hands, fingers laced tightly, as though holding onto each other could keep them anchored in this storm.

Their signs read, *Debt is Not Freedom* and *We're More Than Profits*.

Just beyond them, a cluster of elderly citizens clutched their signs with trembling hands, some leaning on canes or holding each other for support. Their faces were lined, weary from the years they'd lived and from the struggle they were now forced to endure in what should have been the quiet years of their lives. Bethany overheard one of them—a woman with a cane decorated in American flags—murmuring to her friend, "This isn't the country I grew up in."

Near Bethany, LGBTQ youth held signs, their eyes defiant as they chanted. Some of them had driven for hours, slept in their cars, sacrificed whatever they could to stand here and make their voices heard. They wore pride flags draped around their shoulders like armor, their faces resolute, even as they stole wary glances at the line of officers blocking the Capitol steps.

It was Bethany's first protest. Her heart was pounding, the sound of it mixing with the chants and cries of the crowd around her. She had never been an activist, never imagined she'd be standing here, screaming for her rights, for her life, but the country she had once trusted had turned on her, had turned on all of them. The policies that had swept through the nation had taken everything—her access to healthcare, her job security, her freedom to live as she had once imagined she could. Now, she was here, one voice among thousands, fighting for the rights that had been ripped from her hands.

A loudspeaker crackled to life, cutting through the chants. The crowd fell into a tense silence, all eyes turning toward the line of police that stood like a wall between them and the Capitol.

"This is an unlawful assembly," a voice boomed, cold and mechanical. "You have two minutes to disperse."

Bethany felt a ripple of fear pass through the crowd, but she held her ground, her grip tightening on her sign. She wasn't here to turn back. She was here to be heard. Around her, the chants resumed, louder now, angrier, as though they could drown out the warning. Voices rose together, a single, defiant cry: "We are the people! You can't silence us!"

The officers didn't move, their faces impassive behind their shields. Bethany scanned their ranks, her gaze falling on a young officer near the center. He looked barely older than some of the college students standing beside her, his face pale, his eyes darting nervously as he scanned the crowd. She saw him hesitate, a flicker of doubt in his gaze as he took in the faces around him—the elderly woman with her cane, the young couple holding hands, the mothers clutching pictures of children lost to a broken healthcare system.

But then his gaze hardened, his face disappearing behind his shield as he straightened, falling back in line.

The loudspeaker crackled again, and the voice continued, its tone cold, devoid of empathy. "You have one minute to disperse."

The response was immediate—a roar of defiance that shook the ground beneath them. People surged forward, hands raised, chanting louder, their voices merging into a single, desperate plea. Bethany felt the energy around her, the power of thousands of voices rising as one, demanding to be heard. She raised her sign higher, her voice merging with the chorus, her heart pounding in her chest.

But beneath the defiance, she could feel the fear. The crowd was on edge, a tightly wound coil ready to snap. She glanced at the line of officers, saw their hands tightening on their shields, saw the glint of riot gear, the barrels of tear gas canisters waiting to be fired. She could feel the tension thick in the air, pressing down on her, suffocating, as though they were all standing on the edge of a cliff, waiting to see who would fall first.

Beside her, a young man with a rainbow flag draped over his shoulders was chanting, his voice strong, determined. He turned to Bethany, his eyes bright with a fierce kind of hope. "They can't ignore us forever," he said, his voice filled with conviction.

Bethany nodded, but her heart was heavy with doubt. She wanted to believe him, wanted to believe that their voices could change something, could make a difference. But as she looked at the faces of the officers, at the blank, unfeeling stares of the government they were standing against, she felt a cold, creeping fear settle in her chest.

The loudspeaker crackled one last time. "This is your final warning."

The response was a thunderous roar, a collective shout that rose above the silence, above the fear. "We will not be silenced!"

And in that moment, something shifted. The crowd surged forward, a wave of bodies pressing against the line of officers, voices rising in anger, in desperation. Bethany felt herself being pushed forward, her sign held high as she stumbled, caught in the surge of people around her. The officers braced themselves, shields raised, their faces grim as the crowd pressed closer.

And then, without warning, a canister of tear gas was fired, arcing through the air before landing in the center of the crowd. The hiss of gas filled the air, and the crowd broke, screams mixing with the acrid sting of the gas as people stumbled back, their eyes watering, their throats burning.

Bethany coughed, her vision blurred as she tried to cover her mouth, tried to shield herself from the gas that filled the air around her. She saw people falling, hands clutching their faces, their voices choked by the gas. She stumbled, her hand reaching out blindly, searching for something to hold onto, something to ground her.

But the chaos only grew, the crowd breaking as more canisters were fired, the hiss of gas mixing with the cries of the protesters. She saw the young man beside her, his face streaked with tears, his rainbow flag clutched tightly in his hand as he was shoved back, his voice lost in the chaos.

The officers began to advance, their shields raised, their batons out, pushing the crowd back with brute force. Bethany felt herself being pushed, shoved, her body jostled by the panicked mass of people around her. She clutched her sign, her fingers numb, her heart pounding with fear, with anger, with a desperation she had never known.

She saw a mother clutching her child, shielding him with her body as they were shoved back, her face etched with fear, with a helplessness that mirrored Bethany's own. She saw an elderly man fall, his cane clattering to the ground, his voice lost in the roar of the crowd.

And then, over the chaos, she heard it—a gunshot, sharp and deafening, cutting through the air like a knife. The gunshot shattered the air, its sharp crack slicing through the chaos, and for one brief, agonizing moment, the world seemed to stand still. Bethany felt her heart lurch, her mind blank with shock as she processed the sound, the reality of it sinking into her bones. Around her, the crowd froze, a collective breath held in terror, in disbelief.

And then, as if on cue, the chaos erupted anew. People screamed, a shrill, piercing sound that filled the square as the crowd surged backward, a frantic, desperate wave of bodies fighting to escape the advancing line of officers. Bethany stumbled, nearly tripping over someone's fallen sign, her vision blurred by tears and the lingering sting of tear gas. She felt hands pushing, pulling, bodies pressing in from all sides as people scrambled to get away, to find safety in a place where there was none.

More gunshots rang out, each one sending a fresh wave of panic through the crowd. Bethany saw people fall, their bodies crumpling to the ground, their hands reaching out in silent pleas as the line of officers moved forward, unrelenting, a wall of force driving the crowd back. She could see the fear in their eyes now, the raw, unfiltered terror that mirrored her own. The thin line between law and chaos had been shattered, replaced by something primal, something ugly.

Ahead of her, a young woman holding a camera stepped forward, her voice shaking as she shouted, "This is the United States! You can't do this!" Her words were barely audible over the noise, but her face was resolute, her eyes blazing with a courage that seemed almost reckless.

Bethany recognized her from the news—Diana Chen, a journalist who had been covering the protests for weeks, her reports raw and unfiltered, a voice that had dared to speak the truth when so many others had turned away. She raised her camera, her gaze steady, her hands trembling as she focused on the line of officers, on the chaos unfolding before her.

But then, before Bethany could even process what was happening, a shot rang out. Diana's body jerked, her camera slipping from her hands as she crumpled to the ground, her face frozen in shock, in betrayal. The camera hit the pavement with a hollow thud, a final, brutal punctuation to her last report.

Bethany's heart twisted, a sick, cold feeling settling in her stomach as she watched the lifeless form of the woman who had been their voice, their witness. The crowd around her screamed, a collective howl of outrage, of grief, of disbelief that this could happen, here, on the steps of their Capitol, to one of their own. The freedom of the press, the right to be heard—it had all been silenced in a single, merciless instant.

Bethany's vision blurred with tears, her body numb as she watched Diana's blood pool on the pavement, mingling with the dust, with the footprints of the people who had once looked to her for hope. She felt a scream building in her throat, a raw, guttural sound that she forced down, her fingers digging into the edges of her sign, her knuckles white with the force of her grip.

The officers advanced, their faces masked, unfeeling, their movements mechanical as they closed in on the crowd. Around her, people were beginning to fall back, stumbling over each other, their voices hoarse with fear, with panic, as they scrambled to get away. But the officers didn't relent. They raised their batons, swinging with a brutality that sent bodies tumbling to the ground, their cries lost in the roar of the chaos.

Beside her, Bethany saw a young officer hesitate, his baton raised, his face twisted with something that looked like doubt, like guilt. His gaze met hers for a brief moment, and she saw the flicker of humanity, the crack in the armor that had been forced upon him.

But before he could move, before he could make a choice, another officer grabbed him, shoving him back in line. Bethany watched as his face hardened, his eyes dull with resignation as he fell back into step, his baton raised, his expression unreadable.

Around her, the cries of the wounded filled the air, a symphony of pain and fear that seemed to echo through the city, reverberating off the walls, filling every empty space. She saw people falling, their bodies trampled by the surging crowd, their hands reaching out in silent pleas that went unanswered. She saw mothers clutching their children, shielding them with their bodies as they stumbled back, their faces etched with horror, with a helplessness that mirrored her own.

Bethany's mind was a whirlwind of fear, of anger, of a desperation that threatened to consume her. She wanted to scream, to fight, to do something, anything, to stop the madness, but her body was frozen, her feet rooted to the ground as she watched the world unravel around her.

And then, without warning, another shot rang out, followed by another, and another, each one a brutal reminder of the cost of their defiance, of the price they were paying for standing here, for daring to speak out. She saw people fall, their bodies hitting the ground with sickening thuds, their blood staining the pavement, a stark, unforgiving contrast against the gray stone.

The officers began to arrest people, their hands reaching out, grabbing whoever they could, their faces impassive as they dragged people away, their cries for mercy, for justice, falling on deaf ears. Bethany saw a woman, her face bruised, her arms twisted behind her back, her voice raw as she screamed for her daughter, her cries drowned out by the relentless march of the officers.

Bethany's heart pounded, her mind racing as she tried to make sense of the horror unfolding before her. She wanted to run, to escape, but she couldn't tear her gaze away, couldn't abandon the people who had become her family, her allies in this fight. She watched as they were pulled away, one by one, their voices growing fainter, their bodies disappearing into the sea of blue uniforms, swallowed up by a system that saw them as nothing more than numbers, as threats to be neutralized.

She stumbled back, her feet slipping on the blood-slicked pavement, her mind numb with fear, with grief, with a rage that burned deep in her soul. She felt a hand on her shoulder, turning to see a young woman, her face streaked with tears, her voice a broken whisper.

"Run," she said, her voice shaking. "They're coming for all of us."

But Bethany couldn't move, couldn't tear herself away. She looked back at Diana's body, at the blood pooling around her, at the shattered camera that lay beside her, a silent testament to the price of truth.

And as she stood there, frozen, the world around her descended into darkness, the sound of gunfire echoing in her ears, a brutal reminder that they had been silenced, that their voices had been erased, that the dream of freedom, of justice, had been snuffed out in a single, merciless moment. Bethany's legs finally moved, her body jolting back to life as the weight of survival crashed down on her. She turned, her shoes skidding on the blood-soaked pavement, her lungs burning as she tried to pull in breaths thick with tear gas and the bitter sting of smoke. Behind her, the chaos roared on, a relentless symphony of gunshots, screams, and desperate pleas echoing into the night. She could barely think, her mind a muddled whirl of images: Diana's fallen body, the tear-streaked faces of the young couple she'd stood beside, the elderly woman with her flag cane left crushed beneath a stampede of fleeing protesters.

Her heart thundered in her chest, pounding against her ribcage with a fear so raw it felt like it might tear her apart. She dodged past people scrambling in every direction, some screaming, some silent in shock, faces blank with the horror of what was happening. The Capitol, once a symbol of hope, loomed over them, a stark silhouette against the fiery glow of the streetlights, an indifferent witness to the destruction unfolding at its feet.

Bethany tripped, her knees slamming against the concrete as she fell, her palms scraping against the rough ground. Pain shot through her, sharp and immediate, but she pushed herself up, forcing her body forward, away from the gunfire, from the batons, from the gloved hands that reached out to pull more protesters down.

She stumbled past an officer, his helmet askew, his riot gear battered, as he dragged a young man in handcuffs through the crowd. The young man's face was bloodied, his eyes glazed with shock as he looked up, meeting Bethany's gaze for a fleeting moment. In that second, she saw everything—the confusion, the betrayal, the haunting realization that he was being silenced in the very place where he should have been protected. And then he was gone, swallowed up in the wave of bodies as the officer hauled him away.

A fresh round of gunfire erupted, the shots sending a new surge of panic through the crowd. Bethany flinched, her heart seizing as she heard the cries of those caught in the line of fire, their voices piercing through the darkness, filled with a pain that was almost too much to bear. She forced herself forward, her legs numb, her mind reeling with the brutality of it all.

Ahead of her, she saw the silhouette of an officer raising his baton, bringing it down on a man huddled on the ground, his hands covering his head as he tried to shield himself from the blows. Bethany's throat tightened, a scream clawing its way up, but she choked it back, terror flooding her senses as she realized that any sound, any movement could make her a target.

Around her, people were being rounded up, shoved into waiting vans, their cries muffled as the doors slammed shut. She watched, helpless, as the last remnants of the protest were snuffed out, the once-defiant voices reduced to silence, the fight stripped from them in a merciless, unyielding display of force.

And then she saw it—the news vans, lined up on the outskirts of the square, cameras trained on the carnage, reporters standing frozen, their faces pale, their expressions a mix of shock and horror. But as she watched, officers descended upon them, tearing cameras from hands, shoving journalists into the crowd with ruthless efficiency. Bethany's stomach churned as she realized what was happening—the truth was being erased, the evidence of their suffering, their resistance, was being silenced in real time.

One of the journalists, a woman with a microphone still clutched in her hand, tried to resist, shouting, "People need to see this! The world needs to know!" But her voice was cut off as an officer grabbed her, his grip brutal as he ripped the microphone from her hands, tossing it to the ground. The last fragments of their story, their struggle, crushed beneath the heel of a boot.

Bethany's vision blurred, tears streaming down her face as she stumbled forward, the realization settling over her like a shroud. They were alone. No one was coming to help, no one would see the footage, would hear their cries. The truth was being buried here, tonight, along with the bodies, the lives shattered by a government that had turned on its own.

She looked back one last time, her eyes lingering on the Capitol, on the place that had once represented freedom, justice, hope. And she felt a hollow ache in her chest, a grief so deep it threatened to consume her, to pull her under. She wanted to scream, to cry out for the lives stolen, for the dreams crushed beneath the weight of authority. But her voice was gone, her throat raw, her spirit broken.

As she turned to flee, as she disappeared into the shadows of the city, the echoes of the massacre followed her, haunting her every step. The faces of those she'd lost, of the friends she'd marched beside, of the people who had dared to hope, who had believed in a better world, lingered in her mind, a reminder of what they had fought for, of what they had sacrificed.

And she knew, with a certainty that chilled her to the bone, that this was only the beginning. The world they had known was gone, erased in a single, violent act of betrayal. And as she ran, as the darkness swallowed her whole, she carried with her the last remnants of their defiance, a spark of resistance that would one day, somehow, rise from the ashes.

But tonight, all she could do was run, her heart heavy with grief, her body trembling with the weight of a massacre that would never be forgotten, that would haunt the nation for generations to come.

NINETEEN

The faint crackle of static filled the air, followed by a heavy silence. And then, after a beat, a voice came through, low and resonant, the words thick with ten years' worth of grief, anger, and unyielding resolve.

"This is Glen Farris," the voice began, layered with sorrow and conviction, the tremor of a man who had witnessed the disintegration of his country and refused to let the story die. "If you're hearing this, you've found one of the last places where this story can be told. I'm broadcasting from the shadows, across a fractured land. Ten years—it's been ten years since Project 2025 reshaped everything we thought we knew. Ten years since the promises of a new era turned into the nightmare that grips us now."

He paused, letting the words settle like dust over the quiet. He imagined those on the other end, listening: families huddled in darkened rooms, parents who could still remember when life was different, children raised in a world of whispers. They were all clinging to this faint signal, to a voice that would not be silenced.

"People call it *The Decade of Defeat* now," he said, his tone barely above a whisper. "And they're not wrong. The places I've been, the faces I've seen… there's a hollowness, a silence that's settled over everything. Entire towns look like graveyards of forgotten dreams, ghostly remnants of what once was. Places that used to be filled with laughter, life, hope—now abandoned, empty, silent."

His voice dropped, thick with sorrow and pain.

"When they rolled back protections, when they said they were 'returning America to its roots,' they promised a new kind of freedom. A freedom for the people. They said it was about giving us control, about letting us choose our destiny. But all I see is suffering, desperation. The only freedom we've been given is the freedom to survive on our own, to be forgotten."

He took a steadying breath, the pain in his voice unfiltered and raw.

"Maybe you remember the beginning," he continued, voice softening. "The promises of security, prosperity, of a government that would protect us. But I was there, I was in D.C. the day it all turned. I was there when citizens, just like you and me, were met with force, with violence, with a silence that settled over the Capitol like a shroud. They called it *The Massacre of 2025*. They said it was 'necessary.' But tell that to the people who watched their friends, their children, their neighbors, bleed on those steps."

His voice caught, as if even now, the memory of that day weighed too heavily to bear.

"Since that day, since that turning point, I've been walking this country, slipping through the cracks, gathering the stories of those left behind. And what I've seen… it's not the America I once believed in. Entire towns have emptied, schools and clinics abandoned. People are terrified, ashamed, hollow. I've seen mothers weep over empty shelves, watched fathers cling to unpaid bills, promising children a future they no longer believe in."

Glen's voice grew quieter, edged with a simmering grief. "They sold us a future that's become a prison. There are elderly men and women, people who fought for this country, left to ration medication they can barely afford, forced into shelters that once housed the homeless, now housing those who once believed they'd be taken care of. This isn't freedom. It's abandonment. It's betrayal."

He paused, his words sinking into the silence, the grief shared by those listening, each sentence echoing what many had felt but never voiced.

"And it's not just the veterans," he said, his tone darkening with quiet rage. "It's our children, too. I've walked through towns where schools are gone, where learning has become a privilege. Children are taught by parents who can barely keep the roof over their heads, young minds forced to give up dreams of college, of something greater. They're told to 'find another way,' as if a future should be a sacrifice they weren't prepared for."

The silence lingered, filled with the unspoken pain of a nation.

"They took away education, health, even clean air. Called it 'freedom to grow,' said it would let businesses flourish. But that's not what I see. I see rivers turning dark, soil that's poisoned, air thick with smoke. I've seen families afraid to let their kids outside, afraid to drink the water, terrified to plant anything in a ground that's betrayed them."

His voice wavered, thick with anger, grief, and something that bordered on hopelessness.

"This isn't freedom," he whispered. "This isn't progress. This is ruin. And as I've moved from town to town, city to city, I've found the same thing—people left behind, forgotten, treated as numbers, as liabilities, in a system that no longer sees them."

He drew in a long, shuddering breath, the silence that followed like a wound, deep and unhealed.

"If you're listening to this," he continued, his voice barely a whisper, "then you know what I'm talking about. You know the pain, the fear, the grief. You've seen the empty shelves, the bare streets, the schools that used to mean something. And you're not alone. We're all feeling this. Every day, every night."

He paused, his voice trembling with sorrow and unspoken rage.

"But maybe, just maybe… there's still something left. There's still something to fight for."

And with that, the static returned, his voice fading into the quiet, leaving those listening to sit with the weight of his words, the echo of a pain that had become theirs to share. he static faded, and Glen's voice returned, sounding more weathered, heavier, as if each word he spoke was a burden he'd carried for too long.

"As I've traveled through this broken country, what hits the hardest isn't the empty buildings or the hollowed-out homes," he continued, his voice thick with sorrow. "It's the faces. The people left to fend for themselves in a world that's forgotten them. I was in a hospital recently—if you can call it that. It was a rundown shelter, barely holding together. People sat in long lines, some clutching their sides in pain, others cradling children too sick to cry."

He paused, his voice catching with the weight of what he had seen. "Doctors who once worked with every resource now have almost nothing. Patients who would have lived, who would have been fine, now left to suffer because there was no other option. People in pain, left untreated, the doors of real hospitals closed to them because they can't pay the price. Can you imagine that? Being turned away, again and again, while you or someone you love is slipping away?"

A deep breath filled the silence, his exhale ragged, his voice a mix of frustration and heartbreak.

"They said this was freedom. They called it efficiency, letting healthcare stand on its own. But what I saw... it was desperation. Mothers clutching sick children, elders leaning on worn canes, faces turned down in shame, in hopelessness. They've turned our pain into profit, our suffering into a transaction. And all we're left with are apologies and empty promises."

He paused, a tremor of anger threading through his voice. "They want us to believe this is normal, that it's just the way things are. But I remember what it used to be like. I remember a time when there was help, when there was a hand to reach out to, when no one had to choose between survival and dignity."

The silence that followed felt like a wound, deep and unhealed, and Glen pushed forward, his words strained with a mix of grief and fury.

"It's not just the hospitals," he continued. "It's the homes, the communities. I've met families forced out of places they lived for generations, told there was no safety net, no help left to give. I met a father once, a proud man who worked his whole life, now sleeping in his truck because his home was taken, because every shelter was full. And still, he tries to smile for his daughter, tries to make her believe it's just temporary."

His voice broke slightly, filled with an emotion he couldn't quite keep contained. "They told us that this was progress. That by taking away the so-called 'crutches' we'd stand on our own. But all I see are people left without homes, without security, without hope."

He paused, his words hanging heavy, filled with unspoken sorrow.

"And then there's the land itself," Glen whispered, his tone darkening. "They called it cutting red tape, unleashing business potential. But I've walked through valleys where the air is thick with smoke, where rivers run black with the runoff of factories given free rein. I've seen farmland turned barren, families told to fend for themselves as the ground they once lived on turned against them."

He exhaled, his voice trembling with the weight of his anger.

"They said it was for the people, but I don't see freedom in poisoned rivers, in sick children, in farmers staring at fields that will never grow again. I see suffering. I see loss. And I see the heartbreak of people who believed, who wanted so desperately to believe, that these promises would help them."

He took a deep breath, steadying himself, letting the silence settle before speaking again.

"I know it's hard to hear. I know it's painful to imagine. But this is our reality. This is the world we've been left with. And for those of you out there who thought this was going to be different, I understand. I've met people who believed it, who trusted those words, those promises. But we can't pretend anymore. We can't keep our heads down, hoping it'll all go away."

His voice softened, filled with a quiet, simmering rage.

"This isn't about politics anymore. This is about life. About a country that's been left to rot, about people who deserve better, who deserve to be seen, to be heard. And if you're listening to this, if you're feeling what I'm saying, then know this—you're not alone.

We're out here. We're hurting, but we're here. And together, maybe there's still something worth fighting for."

The crackle of static returned, his voice slipping away, leaving behind the echo of his words, the quiet, fierce hope of a man who refused to let his country be erased. The static returned, then faded, leaving Glen's voice alone in the silence, growing wearier but still holding firm, like a hand reaching out through the dark.

"I've traveled through this country for ten years," he began again, each word carrying the weight of the years and the countless lives he'd encountered. "And what I've seen… it's beyond words, beyond belief. I was there in the Midwest, in towns that once thrived, towns where families could count on each other and believed in a better future. But those towns are empty now. Factories shut down, homes abandoned, schools dark and silent."

His voice wavered, thick with the sorrow of every story he'd borne witness to. "Imagine driving through a place where you used to hear children laughing, where you'd see neighbors sitting on their porches, and now it's all gone. You walk down the main street, and it's like a ghost town. Storefronts are boarded up, homes are falling apart. And the people who are left… they're just trying to survive. That's all they have left."

A heavy sigh filled the silence, the sorrow in his voice like a weight that pressed down on the air.

"I met a family there, once. The Bakers. They used to run a little grocery store. It had been in their family for generations—a lifeline to the community, a place where people knew each other's names. But after the tariffs, the supply cuts, the cost of goods… they couldn't keep up. They lost everything. I saw them one last time, living out of their car, trying to make it from one town to the next, looking for work that wasn't there. That's what we've come to."

He paused, his voice softening with quiet despair.

"They took away the safety nets, called them 'burdens on the people.' But all I see are people burdened with loss, with grief, with the weight of a system that turned its back on them. I see parents who can't promise their kids a future, who tell them to hold on, to keep going, even when they don't know where that road leads."

His voice dropped, trembling, filled with anger that had been building over the years, the rage of a man who had seen too much.

"They called it freedom. They said it was for us. But when you have parents lining up at food banks, when you have elders lying awake, wondering if they'll survive another winter, another night… that's not freedom. That's a lie. It's a lie that's stolen from us, that's robbed us of what it means to live, to dream, to be safe in our own homes."

He took a deep, shuddering breath, the emotion seeping into his words.

"And it's not just food, not just shelter. I've seen people, people who once had hope, who once had pride in this country, now reduced to nothing. People who have to beg for what used to be theirs, who have to look their children in the eyes and say, 'I'm sorry, this is all we have.'"

Glen's voice dropped to a whisper, barely audible, filled with sorrow.

"This is what they've done. They've stolen our voices, our rights, our dreams. And they want us to believe that it's normal, that it's just the way things are. But I'm telling you now—it doesn't have to be. It never had to be this way."

He stopped, his breath catching as he struggled to find the words.

"For those of you listening, I want you to know that you're not alone. Even if you're out there, even if it feels like you're the only one left, you're not. We're still here. And if we can hold on, if we can keep each other going, then maybe, just maybe, there's still something worth fighting for."

He let the silence settle, the quiet filled with the unspoken grief of a nation. And then, with a voice that trembled with hope, he spoke again.

"We've lost so much. But as long as we remember what's been taken, as long as we hold each other close, there's still a chance. Don't let them steal that from us. Don't let them take away the last of what we have. Because they can take our homes, our jobs, our rights… but they can't take our spirit. That belongs to us. Always."

The static returned, his voice fading, leaving his words as a beacon in the dark, a call to those who had not yet given up. The static crackled, then faded away, and Glen's voice returned, quieter now, but carrying a depth of conviction that came from years spent witnessing a nation's unrelenting collapse.

"As I sit here, speaking to you, I know there are people out there who feel this too," he began, his voice trembling with the weight of everything he'd seen. "I know you're out there, just trying to get by, wondering if things will ever change, if we'll ever get back what's been lost. And I'm here to tell you—you're not alone in that hope. You're not alone in that fight."

He paused, as if gathering strength, his voice softening with a sadness that was almost unbearable.

"I've spent the last ten years crossing this country, seeing what's been left in the wake of promises that were meant to empower us. They said it would be for us, but what I've seen is a nation bled dry, a people left with empty words and broken lives. And it breaks my heart, because I know… I know this isn't what we fought for. This isn't the America we believed in."

His voice grew quieter, almost a whisper, as he remembered the faces, the towns, the voices that had shared their pain with him.

"I remember a man I met in a shelter," he continued. "A father, holding his little girl. They had nothing, just the clothes on their backs and each other. And he looked at me, this man who'd lost everything, and he said, 'I just want her to be safe. I just want her to have a future.'"

Glen's voice wavered, the memory pressing down on him.

"And that's what's been taken from us—the right to dream, the right to believe that tomorrow will be better. They've stolen our sense of security, our trust, our faith in the systems that were supposed to protect us. And we're left with the aftermath, with the ruins of a promise that was never meant to be kept."

A long silence filled the airwaves, his words hanging heavy, before he spoke again, his voice raw and unguarded.

"I know this is hard to hear. I know it feels like there's nothing left to hold on to. But I want you to know that even now, even in this darkness, there are people who still care. There are people who still believe in a better future, who haven't forgotten what we used to be, what we can still become."

He took a deep breath, his voice steadying as he continued.

"If you're listening to this, if you're feeling this, then know this—you're not alone. We're out here, all of us, scattered but unbroken. And as long as we remember, as long as we refuse to let go, they can't truly defeat us."

His voice softened, the weight of his words pressing down on him like a shroud.

"They can take away our homes, our schools, our safety nets. They can strip us of our rights, our security, our dreams. But they can't take our spirit. They can't take the love we have for each other, the resilience that's been woven into the fabric of who we are. That's ours, and no matter what they do, they can't take that from us."

The silence that followed was deep, profound, as if his words had settled into the hearts of those listening.

"To all of you out there, keep holding on. Keep fighting, keep hoping. Because this isn't the end. Not yet. This is just one chapter, and we—each of us—are the ones who get to decide how it ends."

A pause, his voice barely above a whisper, filled with a quiet, unbreakable strength.

"So hold on to each other. Hold on to that hope, because as long as we have that, there's still a future worth fighting for. We can rise again. We will rise again. And one day, we'll look back on this time—not as the end, but as the moment we remembered who we are, who we've always been, who we can still be."

His voice lingered, the conviction in his words a lifeline in the dark.

"Remember, you're not alone. You are never alone. We will endure. And we will overcome."

The static returned, his voice fading, but his message remained, lingering in the silence—a call to those who still believed, a reminder of resilience, of unity, and of a future that had not yet been written.

IN REFLECTION

To each of you who has journeyed through these pages, I offer my deepest gratitude. Together, we've explored lives shaped by survival—mothers, veterans, students, and workers—who find themselves navigating a world where compassion has frayed, where personal rights are cast aside under the weight of authority. These are not just imagined struggles; they reflect real vulnerabilities, a glimpse into the fractures we risk if we abandon the values that bind us.

This anthology was written out of grief, anger, and a profound hope—that these shadows will never become our reality. These are cautionary tales, yes, but more than that, they are reminders of what's at stake when we grow indifferent, when we accept the erosion of protections, of justice, and of care. Societies do not collapse overnight; they unravel in quiet moments of apathy, in silent acquiescence to "progress" that overlooks the humanity it claims to serve. The stories here are a testament to the resilience of those left to bear these losses and a warning to us all.

At the heart of these narratives is a truth: the strength of a people is not so easily broken. It is not the systems or the mandates that make a nation strong, but the willingness of its people to stand up for one another, to protect the threads of humanity that connect us. Let us not become a people divided, reduced to isolated figures on separate paths. Instead, let us hold fast to the small but vital actions of empathy, unity, and care that prevent us from falling apart.

As readers, you carry this message with you now: the power to hold these warnings close, to let them shape how we act, choose, and care for one another. We are not bystanders in this story. Together, we define its course, carrying the responsibility to ensure these futures remain fiction. By choosing kindness over convenience, justice over complacency, and unity over division, we not only honor ourselves but also those who will come after.

May we write our future with courage, with conviction, and with an unwavering commitment to one another. Thank you—for reading, for bearing witness, and for carrying these echoes forward.

-   Brett